Mikhail Bakhtin: The Dialogical Principle

April 3, 1985

New Haven

Theory and History of Literature
Edited by Wlad Godzich and Jochen Schulte-Sasse

Mikhail Bakhtin
The Dialogical Principle

Tzvetan Todorov

Translated by Wlad Godzich

Theory and History of Literature, Volume 13

University of Minnesota Press, Minneapolis

The University of Minnesota Press
gratefully acknowledges assistance to translation
and publication of this book by the
Georges Lurcy Charitable and Educational Trust.

Published by the University of Minnesota Press,
2037 University Avenue Southeast, Minneapolis MN 55414
Printed in the United States of America
Originally published in Tzvetan Todorov, *Mikhaïl Bakhtine: le principe dialogique
suivi de Écrits du Cercle de Bakhtine*, copyright ©1981 by Éditions du Seuil, Paris.

Library of Congress Cataloging in Publication Data

Todorov, Tzvetan, 1939-
    Mikhail Bakhtin: the dialogical principle.
    (Theory and history of literature; v. 13)
    Translation of: Mikhaïl Bakhtine.
    Bibliography: p.
    Includes index.
    1. Bakhtine, M. M. (Mikhail Mikhailovich), 1895-1975.
I. Title. II. Series.
PG2947.B3T613 1984   801'.95'0947   84-3636
ISBN 0-8166-1290-0
ISBN 0-8166-1291-9 (pbk.)

The University of Minnesota
is an equal-opportunity
educator and employer.

Contents

Translator's Note

Citations from Bakhtin are indicated as follows: The first of the two numbers in the parentheses following a citation is to the number of the work listed in the Chronological List of the Writings of Bakhtin at the back of the book. The second number refers to the page within that book.

All the translations in this book from the writings of Bakhtin and his circle are translated from the Russian original.

Introduction

One could praise Mikhail Bakhtin, without too many qualms, on two counts: that he is the most important Soviet thinker in the human sciences and the greatest theoretician of literature in the twentieth century. There is in fact a certain interdependence between these two accolades: not that one need be a Soviet citizen to excel in literary theory (although the Russian tradition in this field is probably richer than that of any other country), but rather because a genuine theoretician of literature must bring within the scope of his considerations areas other than literature: his specialty, if the word can still be used, is not to be a specialist. Conversely (who knows?), an interest in literature is perhaps a requirement for specialization in the human sciences.

Certainly, such is Bakhtin's case. Primarily a theoretician of texts (in the broad sense of the term, extending beyond "literature"), he saw himself forced by the need to shore up his theories to make extensive forays into psychology and sociology; he returned from them with a unitary view of the entire area of the human sciences, based on the identity of their materials: texts, and of their method: interpretation, or as he would rather put it, *responsive understanding*.

Bakhtin paid particular attention to the sciences of language. In the early twenties, two opposite positions were current: on the one hand, stylistic criticism that cared only for individual expression; on the other, emergent structural linguistics (Saussure), which focused on *langue*, the abstract grammatical form at the expense of other areas of language. Bakhtin's privileged object lies between the two: human utterance as the product of the interaction of *langue* and the context of the utterance—a context that belongs to history. Contrary to the beliefs of both linguists and stylisticians, utterance is neither individual nor infinitely variable and, as such, somehow beyond knowing; it can, and indeed must, become the object of inquiry of a new science of language that Bakhtin will call Translinguistics. The sterile dichotomy of form and content can be overcome in this way, and the formal analysis of ideologies can begin.

The most important feature of the utterance, or at least the most neglected, is its *dialogism*, that is, its intertextual dimension. After Adam, there are no nameless objects nor any unused words. Intentionally or not, all discourse is in dialogue with prior discourses on the same subject, as well as with discourses yet to come, whose reactions it foresees and anticipates. A single voice can make itself heard only by blending into the complex choir of other voices already in place. This is true not only of literature but of all discourse, and Bakhtin finds himself forced to sketch out a new interpretation of culture: culture consists in the discourses retained by collective memory (the commonplaces and stereotypes just as much as the exceptional words), discourses in relation to which every uttering subject must situate himself or herself.

The genre that most favors this polyphony is the novel, and Bakhtin devotes a substantial part of his studies to it. He concentrates on working out the stylistics of the genre in such a way as to simultaneously elucidate its ideological structures and paint an arresting picture of the evolution of narrative prose in Europe. This evolution is dominated by the perpetual, infinitely changing conflict between a tendency toward unification and a contrary tendency that maintains diversity. Later, this analysis is extended to the study of the spatio-temporal models (chronotopes) characteristic of various narrative subgenres, and a structural thematics is added to the stylistics. Bakhtin thus develops what could be called a "Poetics of the Utterance."

The conflict between the two tendencies is ultimately won by the impulse toward diversity, and Dostoevsky's novels are its crowning achievement. The latter are not merely the subject matter of Bakhtin's first published book, but a source of constant inspiration. That is why Bakhtin's reflection on the novel turns into a form of anthropology, and the theory of literature once again exceeds its limits because of its accomplishments: it is the human being itself that is irreducibly heterogeneous; it is human "being" that exists only in dialogue: within being one finds the other. This anthropology is articulated around the same set of values that already governed, for Bakhtin, the history of literature, translinguistics, and the methodology of the human sciences: foremost, there is always becoming, incompletion, dialogue. Let us recall that the word "problem," or one of its synonyms, appears in the title of Bakhtin's major texts (unfortunately it tends to disappear in the translations): *Problems of the Poetics of Dostoevsky, Questions of Literature and Aesthetics, The Problem of the Text. . . .*

Bakhtin's thought is rich, complex, and fascinating, but access to this thought is particularly difficult, even though, in and of itself, it is not obscure. The reasons for this difficulty are multiple.

The first is bound up with history, but not so much the history of the writing of his texts as that of their publication. Two specific circumstances mark this history. The first is that in the five years preceeding the publication of his first book, Bakhtin published nothing under his own name, while during the same period several works appeared that were inspired or even written by him but signed by his friends V. N. Voloshinov and P. Medvedev. This fact was unknown until quite recently (1973), and the ensuing debate concerning the actual identity of the author of these books is not about to die down.

Second, during the course of his subsequent career, Bakhtin wrote without thought of publication (with the exception of the work on Dostoevsky). The book on Rabelais saw the light of day twenty-five years after having been written. It is only after Bakhtin's death (1975) that important texts, dating from different periods of his life, were published: a first collection was supervised by the author; the second was edited by the holders of the manuscripts.

This situation creates two types of difficulties, the first purely material. Texts published in the twenties have long been unavailable, especially to scholars outside the Soviet Union, though the situation is not much better for those who live in it. Medvedev and Voloshinov both disappeared in the thirties; as a result, their books are extremely rare. With the unpublished materials, especially those coming out nowadays, the question is a little different: we do not know from what ensemble they have been drawn, nor do we know what the whole body of Bakhtin's written (and oral but transcribed) production looks like.

In addition, nonpublication (or publication delayed or carried out under pseudonyms) has some influence on the internal organization of these texts. Although Bakhtin's thought is remarkably stable in its

basic choices over the years, its general system is not easily appre-
hensible from the published texts, especially from those that appeared
in his lifetime. In the work not meant for immediate publication,
that is, not written with a new reader in mind—in the sense of a reader new to the work at hand—there is no attempt to articulate among
themselves the various pieces of the system. To rely on the two books
on Dostoevsky and Rabelais—and that was all that readers of Bakhtin
had until his death—could lead to gross errors of interpretation, since
what turned out to be two small peaks of an iceberg were taken for
the whole. Indeed the very link between the two was not intelligible.
In the (characteristically incomplete) project of a preface to the
1975 collection, Bakhtin emphasizes this concern:

> The cohesion of an idea in becoming (in development). Hence a certain internal
> incompletion of many of my thoughts. But I don't want to turn this shortcom-
> ing into a virtue: in my works, there is also considerable incompletion, incom-
> pletion not of thought but of its expression, its exposition. . . . My penchant
> for variation and a plurality of terms to name the same phenomenon. The
> multiplicity of perspectives. The convergence with the distant without any in-
> dication of the intermediate links (38:360).

These statements are not exaggerations. Even if one should seek to
preserve the "internal incompletion," there would remain much
work to be done to bring the expression to completeness, to identify
all the synonymies and polysemies, and to restore the missing links.

In my sketching of the difficulties that await Bakhtin's readers, I
have been taking for granted a knowledge of Russian, whereas, in
point of fact, it is in translation that Western readers first become
acquainted with his writings, and therein lies the second great difficulty. Translations do exist, but I am not sure we should derive any
solace from that fact. Having practiced the craft of translator myself,
I shall refrain from taking my colleagues to task for occasional lapses
that, in any case, are unavoidable. However, what I find alarming in
this instance is that Bakhtin has been translated by individuals who
did not know or did not understand this system of thought, though
I will concede that this is no easy matter. As a result, key concepts,
such as *discourse, utterance, heterology, exotopy,* and many others,
are rendered by misleading "equivalents" or even simply dropped altogether by a translator more concerned with the avoidance of repetition or obscurity. In addition, the same Russian word is not translated in the same way by the various translators, a fact that may cause
the Western reader undue and uncalled-for difficulty. One can but
admire the power of Bakhtin's thought for having nonetheless

managed to find a way of reaching its Western admirers (they do exist).

It is the conjunction of these two facts—the importance of Bakhtin's thought and the difficulty of its access—that has moved me to write this book, and, by the same occasion, it has also determined the form of my project. The foremost lacuna I attempt to fill is quite elementary, yet fundamental: how to make Bakhtin readable in our tongue. I can't quite assert that this text is really my own: just as Jean Starobinski made it possible for us to read Saussure's work on the anagrams, I would like, in a different context and with difficulties of another order, to present Bakhtin's ideas by constructing a kind of montage, halfway between anthology and commentary, where my sentences would not be quite my own. I have obviously retranslated all of the texts cited. Without forgetting that even a minimal commentary can cause distortions, I believe that my name could be added to the psyeudonyms—but are they pure pseudonyms?—used by Bakhtin.

For this reason, I have refrained in principle from entering into a dialogue with Bakhtin: the first voice must be heard before the dialogue can begin. Nor have I taken account here of the reactions, and they have been numerous in the West, occasioned by the first publications: almost all are based on (excusable) misunderstandings. I have also, with some exception, avoided comparing Bakhtin's thought with that of his successors, whereas I have often inquired into his sources. Bakhtin's work is already quite diverse and need not be burdened with further association of ideas. It is undeniable that on several scores Bakhtin's ideas appear especially relevant since they prefigure, or even supersede, the assertions of authors esteemed today. Such convergences remain implicit in principle, in my text; they may have influenced my reading of Bakhtin, but their discussion has no place here.[1]

Mikhail Bakhtin: The Dialogical Principle

Chapter One
Biography

Our main source concerning Bakhtin's life is a note published at the beginning of a *Festschrift* dedicated to Bakhtin, which appeared in the Soviet Union in 1973;[1] I can only summarize it here, adding details drawn from other sources.

Mikhail Mikhailovich Bakhtin was born in 1895 in Orel, in an impoverished aristocratic family; his father was a bank clerk. He spent his childhood in Orel, and his adolescence in Vilnius and Odessa. He studied philology at the University of Odessa and later in Petrograd, graduating in 1918. He taught elementary school, first in the small provincial town of Nevel' (1918-1920), and then, after 1920, in Vitebsk, where he was married in 1921. In Nevel', a first circle of friends was formed;[2] it included Valerian Nikolaevich Voloshinov (1894 or 1895-1936), a poet and musicologist; Lev Vasilievich Pumpian'ski (1891-1940), a philosopher and literary scholar; the pianist M. B. Yudina (1899-1970); the poet B. N. Zubakin (1894-1937); and the philosopher Matvei Isaevich Kagan (1889-1937). The last-named began to play the role of initiator; he had just returned from Germany, where he had studied philosophy in Leipzig, Berlin, and Marburg; he was a disciple of Hermann Cohen, and had attended Cassirer's lectures. Kagan organized an initial informal group that took on the name of "Kantian Seminar." In addition to this private activity, the members of the circle participated in public debates and gave formal talks. The local paper *Molot (Hammer)* relates, for example, the proceedings of a debate on the topic "God and Socialism"; it is of some interest not only because it provides a rare insight into the intellectual ambience of the Soviet Union then, but also because it gives an indication of Bakhtin's interest in religious subjects:

In his talk in defense of the muzzle of obscurity that is religion, comrade Bakhtin floated up in the clouds or even higher. In his remarks, there was not to be found a single living example, drawn from life or from the history of mankind. At some points he did recognize, and even expressed appreciation of, socialism, but he complained of, and worried about, the fact that socialism had no care for the dead (as if there weren't enough services for the dead!), and that, accordingly, in some future time, the people would not forgive us such neglect. . . . Listening to his words one could form the general impression that this entire buried host, reduced to powder as it is, would shortly arise from its tombs and sweep from the face of the earth all the Communists and the Socialism they promote. Comrade Gutman spoke fifth. . . . (December 13, 1918, quoted in [43]).

After Bakhtin's move (and Kagan's departure, first for Petrograd and the Orel), the circle reformed in Vitebsk, with Voloshinov and Pumpian'ski as well as some new additions: the critic Pavel Nikolaevich Medvedev (1891-1938); the musicologist I. I. Sollertinski; the painter Marc Chagall belongs to the same milieu. Bakhtin taught literature and aesthetics. Afflicted since 1921 with a chronic osteomyelitis that eventually required the amputation of a leg in 1938, Bakhtin returned to Petrograd in 1924 where he took up again with his friends Voloshinov, Pumpian'ski, and Medvedev. A third circle was formed; it included this time the poet N. Klinev; the novelist K. Vaginov; the Indic scholar M. Tubianski; the musicologist I. Tubianski; and the biologist and historian of science I. Kanaev. The "Kantian Seminar" resumed its activities. Bakhtin supported himself from odd jobs. In 1929 he published a book: *The Problems of Dostoevsky's Work*; it is known that an early version, probably quite different from the published one, had been completed as early as 1922. In the same year, 1929, Bakhtin was arrested, for reasons that remain unknown but were most likely related to his ties with Orthodox Christianity. It was indeed for such a reason that his friend Pumpian'ski was arrested in 1928; in 1926, writing to Kagan, who lived then in Moscow, he described the meetings of the circle thus: "All these years, and especially this one, we have kept busy dealing with theology. The circle of our closest friends remains the same: M. B. Yudina, M. M. Bakhtin, M. I. Tubianski and myself" (43). Bakhtin was condemned to five years in a concentration camp to be spent in Solovki; for health reasons, however, his sentence was commuted to exile in Kazahkstan.

From 1930 on he worked at clerical jobs in various institutions in the small town of Kustanaj on the border of Siberia and Kazakhstan. In 1936 he was given an appointment to the Teachers' College at Saransk. In 1937, he settled in Kimr, some hundred kilometers from Moscow, where he taught Russian and German in the local secondary school. Occasionally, he participated in the workings of the Literary Institute of the Academy of Sciences in Moscow. He returned to Saransk Teachers' College in 1945 and remained there until his retirement in 1961. His book on Dostoevsky, somewhat enlarged, was republished in 1963. The book on Rabelais, actually a thesis completed in 1940 but defended, with many a difficulty, in 1946, finally appeared in 1965. His health declining, Bakhtin settled in Moscow in 1969. The last years of his life were spent in a retirement home in Klimovsk near Moscow. He died in March 1975, at the age of eighty; his funeral followed Orthodox rites.

Outwardly, Bakhtin's life may have been rather humble, and his professional career indifferent at best, but its significance lies elsewhere: in the intensive labor of writing. For to the two books published in his lifetime many others must be added, which we must consider in two groupings, the posthumous publications and the works published under pseudonyms. During the last ten years of his life, Bakhtin published excerpts from his manuscripts in two rather conformist periodicals: *Voprosy literatury* and *Kontekst*; most of these texts are collected in a volume he arranged himself, even though it saw the light of day only a few months after his death, under the title: *Questions of Literature and Aesthetics*. Other posthumous publications have followed: in 1979 a new collection entitled *Aesthetics of Verbal Creation* appeared.

To give an idea of the way in which Bakhtin undertook projects that he did not complete, here is a list, compiled for the last twenty-five years of his life, of books begun or outlined but never finished. I draw upon the notes published in the most recent collection:

1. A book entitled: *Studies in Translinguistics*, including notably a chapter on the discourse of the other as the object of the human sciences, and another dedicated to the role of contexts that become further and further removed from the original text and their effect on the evolution of the text's interpretation (42:406, 407, 411).

2. A book: *The Genres of Discourse*, probably close thematically to the preceding (42:399).

3. A book: *Studies in Philosophical Anthropology*, a return to some of the themes of the oldest book, written in 1922-1924 (43:406).

4. A new book on Dostoevsky entitled: *Dostoevsky and Sentimentalism. An Essay in Typological Analysis.* (42:406).

5. Another book on Dostoevsky, comparing this time his novels and his journalistic writings, and especially *A Writer's Diary* (42:408).

6. A study of Gogol.

7. A book on the way in which writers seek to find their own personal voice (42:406). It is possible that the last three projects may have been melded into a single one.

There is no guarantee, of course, that this list is exhaustive, nor even that, as of this writing (November 1979), the main portion of Bakhtin's manuscripts have been published.[3]

The matter is even more complex with respect to the pseudonymous (or the presumed pseudonymous) writings. This "controversy" started in 1973 with a statement by V. V. Ivanov—a Soviet semiotician and admirer of Bakhtin, a statement hidden away in footnote 101 of a study of Bakhtin's contribution to the development of semiotics. It read:

The main [osnovnoj] text of works 1-5 and 7 [a book signed Medvedev, two books and three articles signed Voloshinov] is due to M. M. Bakhtin. His disciples V. N. Voloshinov and P. N. Medvedev, under whose names they were published, are responsible only for some minor interpolations; they also modified some parts of these articles and books (or even titles, as in *Marxism and the Philosophy of Language*.) That all of these works are due to the same author—a fact confirmed by witnesses' statements—is something that the text itself forces us to admit.[4]

Roughly at the same time, in an interview published in Polish, Ivanov added the following:

It was easy for Bakhtin to grant the request of two of his friends and disciples, Voloshinov and Medvedev, and to publish his works under their names (with all the changes this required, which they made).[5]

Two other public accounts have been added to Ivanov's statements. The American Slavic specialist T. Winner relates that in a conversation of June 1973, Bakhtin had confirmed that he was the author of these books.[6] A Soviet critic recounts, for his part, that, on the occasion of a visit by Mr. and Mrs. Bakhtin, he placed the book signed by Medvedev on a table. Mikhail Mikhailovich said nothing, but Mrs. Bakhtin, upon sighting the book, exclaimed: "My God, how many times I have copied this book!"[7] Finally, in the notes of Bakhtin's most recent book (1979, posthumous), the following sentence is repeated three times: "The main text of the book is due to M. Bakhtin," with reference to the two books signed Voloshinov and the one bearing Medvedev's name (42:386, 299, 403); and once, the following detail is added: "the book was published under Voloshinov's name" (43:399). Moreover, three articles published by Voloshinov are stated to have been written by Bakhtin: "Discourse in Life and Discourse in Poetry," "The Structure of the Utterance," "On the Boundaries between Poetics and Linguistics," (42:399, 401, 402). On the basis of these testimonies, several translations of these books have recently been published under Bakhtin's name.

I have no new information to contribute to this discussion, but I would like to add some considerations on the significance of the testimonies, as well as a remark on the stakes of correct attribution.

With respect to the first point, let us note the following: Bakhtin never claimed publicly the authorship of the disputed books, not in the late twenties, not in the early sixties. The Polish journalist who interviewed Ivanov also talked to Bakhtin in the course of the same series of interviews; not a word of the encounter is devoted to the issue, even though it is discussed between Ivanov and the journalist. On the other hand, it is quite likely that Bakhtin admitted to authorship in private (Ivanov knew him personally) or let it be believed (by the intermission of his wife). But must we discount this difference of status between the public (and written) word and private utterance? As far as the "witnesses" whom Ivanov never identifies are concerned, one may well doubt their existence. Voloshinov and Medvedev died in the thirties. The secret, if indeed there is one, was well kept in the late twenties, as is shown, for example, by a letter from Pasternak, which will be discussed below. The only witness is Bakhtin himself; but were we even to suppose that he did claim to be the author of these works, what proof do we have that in the twenties his words hid the truth, while in the seventies they revealed it, and not the other way around? For the time being at least, there is no external criterion to establish that Bakhtin wrote these books.

In any case, Ivanov does not assert that Bakhtin wrote them from beginning to end. One time he speaks of "minor interpolations and modifications in some parts," another, of "modifications required by the times," and a third, of "the main text." But how far did these modifications go? At what point does one decide that someone is the co-author of a book rather than its editor? Aren't "interpolations" and "modifications" capable of changing the meaning of the whole? Can it be said that a title has no effect on how a book is read? or shouldn't one rather see in it a key determinant of readers' reception? (It is hard to see, though, how "Marxism" or "Philosophy of language" betray the intention of the text that follows.) And what if these texts as the biographical note (by V. V. Kozhinov) suggests, were simply written "on the basis of conversations with Mikhail Mikhailovich, devoted to problems of philosophy, psychology, philology, and aesthetics?" (Kozhinov/Konkin, p. 6).

Another question arises here. The works signed Medvedev and Voloshinov, but supposedly written by Bakhtin, bear a strong resemblance, both at the level of content and style, to other writings similarly signed but not claimed by the proponents of the pseudonymous authorship thesis. For example, Voloshinov's (Bakhtin's) book *Freudianism* follows another study by Voloshinov, "This Side of the Social," published two years earlier. Voloshinov's study "The Structure of the Utterance," attributed by Ivanov to Bakhtin, is the second of three articles published under the same general title: "Stylistics of Literary Discourse," and it fits perfectly in this series, which looks like the beginning of a book; yet so far no one has come forth to claim Bakhtin as the author of either the first or the third article. Medvedev's book *The Formal Method in Literary Studies* is preceded by his article on "The Current Tasks of Literary-Historical Scholarship," and a new version of the book was published in 1934 under the title *Formalism and the Formalists*; no one has thought of attributing these texts to Bakhtin.

The writings signed Voloshinov and Medvedev but attributed to Bakhtin fit quite well in the body of these authors' writings; on the other side of the coin there are notable differences between the works signed Bakhtin and those that are attributed to him. *The Formal Method in Literary Studies* is far better composed than the other books: the style is clear and simple, the sentences short, the paragraphs frequent, the subheadings numerous, and the chapters well articulated. The books signed Voloshinov are especially dogmatic and tend to be replete with assertions rather than demonstrations. Bakhtin's signed works are characterized by confused composition, repetitions to the point of restatement, and a tendency toward abstraction (due, perhaps, to German philosophy).

Naturally, these surface differences leave untouched a great homogeneity of thought, which is why Ivanov's claim has such a high degree of verisimilitude. But, in the absence of truly convincing external evidence, the comparison between these texts leads to a more guarded conclusion: I would prefer to say that these texts were conceived by the same author(s) but that they were written, in part or in whole, by others.

A second aspect of the controversy that deserves consideration has to do with the very meaning of the totality of Bakhtin's work, and it requires, for its understanding, that we recall the context of the writings in question. The texts listed by Ivanov have a common demoninator: they are polemical and critical. In fact, the three books are as many condemnations and executions: psychoanalysis, formalism in literary studies, contemporary linguistics (especially then nascent structuralism) all draw fire. It has become common to suggest that Voloshinov and Medvedev are responsible for the importation of Marxist terminology into Bakhtin's works, which otherwise may not have been published. A reading of these works does not bear out this allegation. Marxist terminology is not applied from the outside in these books: the three attacks are carried out in the name of Marxism, and they draw from it their very substance. On the other hand, Bakhtin has never published a single polemical text under his own name, and, in his signed works, references to Marxism are quite discrete. Nor is it by chance that his own book on Dostoevsky was condemned on publication by an orthodox Marxist, M. Starinkov, in an article significantly entitled "Polyphonic Idealism" (*Literatura i Marksizm*, 1930; the same periodical had published texts by Medvedev and Voloshinov — or Bakhtin?).

To give an idea of the tone of the polemical writings signed Voloshinov and Medvedev, let us consider some excerpts from their discussion of the Formalists. In 1929, Voloshinov devotes a study to V. V. Vinogradov, a linguist and marginal Formalist, destined to become the official guiding light of Soviet linguistics. He is described in such phrases as "Vinogradov's approach is . . . definitely disastrous," (16:207) and "his way is that of intractable hostility to Marxism" (16:209). In *The Formal Method in Literary Studies*, Medvedev concludes that the Formalists may be appreciated as "worthy enemies" (6:232). But in the second version of the book, published six years later, his language is much harsher:

The undeniable development of Marxist literary studies is by itself a powerful antidote to the Formalist poison (20:7). In its essence — that is as social class — Formalism represents total bourgeois reaction on the battlefield of literary studies. It has always served as a conduit of bourgeois influence (20:8). Although the history of Formalism is ended, and although Formalism has broken down and degenerated, the series of attempts to revive its corpse is far from closed. It is well known that nothing is more deadly than the poison of corpses (20:209).

These sentences are most certainly not Bakhtin's, since the latter had spent the five years prior to their publication contemplating the steppes of Siberia and Kazakhstan. But they do meld perfectly with the argument developed in the central part of the book, with the "main text," which remains the same in the two versions of 1928 and 1934. One must know what it meant at a certain time in the Soviet Union to label someone, in the name of official ideology, an "enemy" (even a "worthy" one) or accuse him of "intractable hostility to Marxism," or of being guilty of "bourgeois reaction." One needs to know this to understand that Bakhtin's overall behavior will be judged quite differently if he is the author of these texts or merely the inspiration of the theory of language to be found in them. Was he perhaps ready, with somewhat more foresight than his friends, to criticize psychoanalysis, linguistics, Formalism, privately, while hesitating to publish these critiques for fear of their consequences? Perhaps he should not have "granted the request of his friends"? It is, after all, in the name of these kinds of writings that the repression of the "supporters of the bourgeois sciences" of psychoanalysis, linguistics, and poetics, took place.

To hold that Bakhtin signs his own name to his positive works while using pseudonyms for the elimination of his enemies, is to turn him into a kind of Dr. Jekyll who uses his Mr. Hyde for his dirty deeds; that is not impossible, but it does not seem to be part of the argument advanced by the pseudonymous authorship camp. This matter has an even more sinister side. During this period of the history of the Soviet Union, the author of polemical writings of this kind ran the risk of becoming himself the target of subsequent polemics: the executioner is quite easily identified as the next victim; one need recall here only the fate of the various heads of the state security apparatus. Voloshinov may well have died of natural causes, but such was not the case of Medvedev. The Formalists' executioner in 1928, he was considered a Formalist himself a few years later. His attack was judged to have been too soft and to have evidenced a connivance with the enemy. The 1934 edition attempted to remedy the situation by having recourse, in the introduction and conclusions, to the vulgar language cited above, but it turned out to be a case of too little, too late. Condemned for ideological deviance, Medvedev was arrested and deported; his biographical note in the Soviet *Short Literary Encyclopedia* ends laconically; "illegally repressed; posthumously rehabilitated." In such a context I would be most loath to deny him the even partial authorship of works for which he died.

My considerations are not meant to refute the thesis of Bakhtin's sole authorship of the disputed texts, but they do give an idea of the stakes of such a thesis. Let us now consider matters from another perspective, which will lead us to examine the substance of these books. The question of an author's relation to his book (or his discourse) receives great attention in Bakhtin's work. One of the theses he advances states that the author is not solely responsible for the content of the discourse he produces; the receiver, at least as imagined by the author, is equally involved in the process: one writes differently for different audiences. The books that concern us were perhaps written by Bakhtin; in that case, they may have been addressed to different recipients: *Freudianism* and *Marxism and the Philosophy of Language* to Voloshinov (Bakhtin became then more of a linguist and more of a Marxist); *The Formal Method in Literary Studies* to Medvedev (and Bakhtin became more forceful, more biting); the *Problems of Dostoevsky's Work* to a larger audience (and Bakhtin became "Bakhtin"). To that extent, even if Medvedev and Voloshinov were no more than addressees, actual or imaginary, of these books, they are entitled, in accordance with Bakhtin's own thinking, to have their name on the cover in lieu of his.

A conclusion seems unavoidable: it is unacceptable to simply erase Voloshinov's and Medvedev's names, and to thus go against Bakhtin's obvious desire not to assume the *publication* of these writings. But it is equally impossible not to take into account the unity of thought evidenced by the whole set of these works, a unity one could attribute, in accordance with the various testimonies, to Bakhtin's influence. I will propose then the adoption of the following typographical convention for these texts: keeping the name under which they have published but following it with a slash and Bakhtin's name: Medvedev/Bakhtin. The slash is chosen specifically for the ambiguity it authorizes: is it a relation of collaboration? of substitution (pseudonym or mask)? or communication (the first name identifying the receiver, and the second, the sender)?[8]

Let us return, after this long but necessary digression, to Bakhtin's biography. With the addition of these four volumes—even if he did not materially write them—to his bibliography, already consisting of the two volumes published in his lifetime and the two published posthumously, an attempt to indicate the main periods of his intellectual biography can be undertaken:

1. Before 1926: writings of a general theoretical nature, conceived in the great German tradition of philosophical aesthetics that goes from Kant to Husserl; Bakhtin himself has sometimes called them "phenomenological" or inquiries into "philosophical ethics." Course on the general history of Russian literature.

2. 1926-1929: methodological and critical writings, aggressively

Marxist, none signed by Bakhtin; this is the "sociological" period. Working out of the ideas that will be the basis of the texts of the next period.

3. 1929-1935: theoretical research on the utterance and on dialogism, from the book on Dostoevsky (first version written as early as 1922) to the "Discourse in the Novel."

4. 1936-1941: reinterpretation of literary history, especially that of the novel; works on the chronotope, *Bildungsroman* (Goethe), and Rabelais. A long article entitled "Satire" meant for *Literary Encyclopedia* belongs to this period, but has never been published.

5. 1942-1952: no text is dated from these years. But the biographical note states that Bakhtin wrote a great deal during the years of his appointment at Saransk Teachers College (1945-1961): "There are articles and reviews published in the local press (they haven't been collected). The bulk [of these texts] awaits publication" (Kozhinov/ Konkin, p. 13). In addition, Bakhtin taught full-time. He offered courses on "Western literature: Antiquity, the Middle Ages, Renaissance, Enlightenment, 19th and 20th Century" (Kozhinov/Konkin, p. 14). He gave "several hundred lectures for the workers of Saransk in factories, plants, schools, and various organizations and institutions" (Kozinov/Konkin, pp. 14-15). It may be supposed that the texts of these courses and lectures are not permanently lost. It is perhaps at this time that he wrote another book, on sentimentalism and literature, whose manuscript has not been preserved (42:407).

6. 1953-1975: revision of older works, and return to the great theoretical and methodological themes of the beginning. In my estimation, the fragments produced in these years, which never do constitute a whole text, are Bakhtin's most remarkable writings.

The existence of these definite periods in Bakhtin's life is undeniable, even if their exact boundaries are at times subject to uncertainty. And yet one can state, at the same time and with equal validity, that, properly speaking, there is no *development* in Bakhtin's work. Bakhtin does change his focus; sometimes he alters his formulations, but, from his first to his last text, from 1922 to 1974, his thinking remains fundamentally the same; one can even find identical sentences written fifty years apart. Instead of development, there is *repetition*, a repetition obviously sectional for the most part, a sifting over and over of the same themes. Bakhtin's writings are more akin to the elements of a series than to the components of a progressively erected construction; each one contains, in a way, the whole of his thought, but it also holds a slippage, a displacement within this same thought, at times barely perceptible yet ultimately most deserving of attention.

That is why I have decided, in my exposition, to privilege systematic perspective over chronological order, although I do rely upon the latter in two respects—insofar as each theme is concerned, if there are changes in Bakhtin's ideas; and in the very order in which the themes are studied: I start with methodological issues, I discuss then his theory of the utterance, and then I proceed to his contribution to literary history. Such a sublation of theory by history is in keeping with Bakhtin's thinking (he writes: "It is only on a concrete historical subject that a theoretical problem can be resolved." 22:198); in fact, it occurs at least twice in his career: the philosophical and theoretical investigations of the twenties end in 1929 in a book devoted to the study of a single author, Dostoevsky; and the vast generalizations on the history of the novel worked out in the thirties lead up to the books on Goethe (1938) and Rabelais (1940). Finally, I end up with the study of a problematic at work in all of Bakhtin's work; I believe it to be the ideological basis of all his research.

These then are the four areas I will examine in turn: epistemology, translinguistics, history of literature, and philosophical anthropology. But it must be borne in mind that this thematic division is no less relative than the periodic one. Bakhtin's epistemology is grounded in his theory of language; his history of literature leads to anthropological reflexion; and the dialogical principle remains his dominant theme whatever the object under scrutiny.

Chapter Two
Epistemology of the Human Sciences

Natural Sciences and Human Sciences

Introducing the notion of *chronotope*, a spatiotemporal complex characteristic of every novelistic subgenre, Bakhtin makes a curious terminological remark:

> The term *chronotope* is used in mathematical biology where it was introduced and adapted on the basis of [Einstein's] theory of relativity. The specific meaning it has come to have there is of little interest to us; we will introduce it here, into literary studies, somewhat like a metaphor (somewhat, but not quite) (23: 234-235).

This "somewhat, but not quite" can set one to think, especially since this type of transferral across fields is far from uncommon in Bakhtin's writings. For example, Dostoevsky's revolution in the field of the novel is compared to that of Einstein.

> The problems encountered by the author and his consciousness in the polyphonic novel are far deeper, and more complex than those to be found in the homophonic (monologic) novel. Einstein's world possesses a far deeper and more complex unity than Newton's; it is a higher level unity, of a qualitatively different order (31:324).

Another comparison between some facts of language and some aspects of the physical world appears occasionally but strategically in his writings.

When cultures and tongues had interanimated each other, language became altogether different; its very quality altered: instead of a Ptolemaic linguistic world, unified, singular, and closed, there appeared a Galilean universe made of a multiplicity of tongues, mutually animating each other (24:429-30).

The Renaissance witnessed a decentered use of language that occurred especially in the novel, which corresponds to the Galilean conception of the world rather than the Ptolemaic. For Bakhtin, this correspondence, which is thus more than a metaphor, can be explained by the fact that the arts and sciences follow the evolution of ideology, hence a "family resemblance" among them. Consequently, Bakhtin will not speak of relations of determination but rather of an "adequation" between these different forms of ideology:

Only a Galilean linguistic consciousness could be adequate to the era of the great astronomical, mathematical, and geographic discoveries that destroyed the finitude and closure of the old universe, the finiteness of mathematical values, and extended the boundaries of the old geographic world, an era—the epoch of the Renaissance and Protestantism—that destroyed the verbal and ideological centralization of the Middle Ages (21:226).

There exists then, between the natural and the human sciences, a historical parallelism that can be explained by their common rootedness in the ideological and the social. However, alongside this first thesis on the unity and homogeneity of the fields of knowledge, there is also a principle of differentiation that separates human and natural sciences. Bakhtin discovers this principle almost by chance while studying the role of *discourse (parole)* in various human activities. Essential in the human sciences, it is of no account in the natural ones:

Mathematical and natural sciences do not acknowledge discourse as an object of inquiry. . . . The entire methodological apparatus of the mathematical and natural sciences is directed toward mastery over *reified objects* that do not reveal themselves in discourse and communicate nothing of themselves. In their practice, knowledge is not bound to the reception and interpretation of discourses or signs coming from the very object to be known.

In the human sciences, as distinct from the natural and mathematical sciences, there arise the specific problems of establishing, transmitting, and interpreting the discourse of others (for example, the problem of sources in the methodology of the historical disciplines). And of course in the philological disciplines, the speaker and his or her discourses are the fundamental objects of inquiry (21: 163-164).

This simple finding justifies after the fact certain hypotheses concerning the very nature of knowledge in the human sciences, and especially in those disciplines that have *discourse* as their object (thus leaving linguistics aside).

In poetics, history of literature (and in the history of ideology in general), or to a considerable extent even in the philosophy of language, no other approach is in fact possible; even the most arid and earthbound positivism cannot treat discourse neutrally as if it were a thing but is forced to engage in talk not only about discourse but with discourse in order to penetrate its ideological meaning, which is attainable only by a form of dialogical understanding that includes evaluation and response (21:164).

This decisive separation between the sciences of nature and those of the spirit, as well as the assertion that the latter's specificity resides in their handling of texts, and therefore in interpretation, obviously recalls the theses first advanced by Dilthey. They are far from unknown to Bakhtin, who subjected them to explicit criticism in *Marxism and the Philosophy of Language*. Here is the summary he gives in that work:

[According to Dilthey] the task of psychology should not be the causal explanation of psychic experiences, as if they were analogous to physiological or physical processes. The task of psychology is to describe with understanding, to analyze and interpret psychic life as if it were a document subject to philological analysis. Only such a descriptive or interpretive psychology can, according to Dilthey, be the basis of the human sciences or, as he calls them, the "sciences of spirit" *(Geisteswissenschaften)* (12:29-30).

That is the very program adopted by Voloshinov/Bakhtin. Bakhtin's critique of Dilthey consists in simply charging the latter with the failure to draw all the consequences of his thesis. (In that respect, Bakhtin was wrong, but he did not have access to Dilthey's then unpublished work.)

For Dilthey, the juxtaposition of psychic experience with discourse is indeed no more than a simple analogy, an illuminating image, actually quite rare in his work. He is far from drawing the necessary consequences from such a comparison (12:30-31).

In a later text, Bakhtin ascertains that Dilthey's and Rickert's formulations are no longer applicable; nonetheless in a very Diltheyan mode, he calls for "the rigorous distinction between understanding and scientific study" (38:349). Bakhtin's goal is actually the radicalization of Dilthey's program, with some subtle shading. He will come to identify two points where the difference between natural and human sciences is precipitated: in their object and in their method (that is, in the knowing subject).

Difference in the Object

The difference in the object is a factual given: the object of the human sciences is a text, in the broad sense of signifying matter.

We are interested in the specificity of the human sciences, which are oriented towards the thoughts, the meanings, the significations, etc., that come from the other, and that are realized and become accessible to the scholar only *sub specie* of the text (30:282). The text, written or oral, is the primary datum of all of these disciplines [linguistics, philology, literary studies] and generally of human and philological sciences (including theologico-philosophical thought at its origin). The text is the *immediate reality* (reality of thought and of experience) within which this thought and these disciplines can exclusively constitute themselves. Where there is no text, there is neither object of inquiry nor thought (30:281).

The object of the human sciences is therefore not just man, but man as producer of texts.

The human sciences are the sciences of man in his specificity, and not the sciences of a *voiceless* thing and a natural phenomenon. Man, in his human specificity, is always expressing himself (speaking), that is always creating a text (though it may remain *in potentia*). Where human being is studied outside of the text and independently of it, we are no longer dealing with the human sciences (but with human anatomy, or physiology, etc. . . .) (20:285).

Both the idea and the distinction it makes were already present in Voloshinov/Bakhtin's first theoretical publication. "Physical and chemical bodies exist outside human society as well, whereas the products of ideological creation develop only within it and for it" (7:246).

Bakhtin will use different formulations to define the object of the human sciences. In the writings of the twenties, he relies on an opposition of venerable antiquity, since it dates from Saint Augustine, between things and signs. In the subsection entitled "The Word as Ideological Sign" of an article signed Voloshinov, the sign is described as that which refers back to something else, in distinction to *things* that are, for their part, intransitive; in further imitation of Augustine, signs are then divided into "already existing" and "specially created." The human sciences are then subdivisions of semiotics. At the same time, Voloshinov/Bakhtin seems to consider as interchangeable the two notions of set of signs (or semiotic) and ideology:

By ideology we will mean the set of reflections and refractions of social and natural reality that is held by the human brain and which the brain expresses and fixes through words, drawings, lines, or whatever signifying [*znakovoj*] form (17:53). *Ideologically*: that is in a sign, a word, a gesture, a graph, a symbol, etc. (17:60).

This idea will be picked up, always in programmatic fashion, in *Marxism and the Philosophy of Language*, and it is still to be found in Bakhtin's very last writings:

The human act is a text *in potentia* (30:286). Scienceof spirit. The spirit, mine as well as the other's, is not a given, like a thing (like the immediate object of the natural sciences); rather, it comes through expression in signs, a realization through "texts," which is of equal value to the self and to the other (30:284).

In a text originally written in 1941, and then returned to in 1974, Bakhtin attempts to define once again the specificity of the human sciences; this time, the opposition is no longer between things and signs, but between things and persons.

Knowledge of the thing and knowledge of the person. They must be depicted as boundaries: the thing, pure and dead, is nothing but externality; it exists only for the other, and it is the other (the knowing subject) who can reveal it entirely, down into its deepest recesses. . . . The second boundary is the thought of the person in presence of the person itself, dialogue, interrogation, prayer (28:409). Two boundaries of thought and praxis or two types of relations (the thing, the person). The deeper the person, that is the closer we edge to the personal boundary, the less applicable any generalizing method; generalization and formalization efface the boundaries between genius and mediocrity. . . . Our *thought* and our *praxis* (not the technical one, but the *moral*, i.e. the set of our responsible acts) take place between two boundaries: the relation to the *thing*, and the relation to the *person. Thingification* and *personification* (40:370).

Another way of stating this would be to say that in the natural sciences we seek to know an *object*, but in the human ones, a *subject*.

The exact sciences are a monological form of knowledge: the intellect contemplates a *thing* and speaks of it.[1] Here, there is only one subject, the subject that knows (contemplates) and speaks (utters). In front of him there is only a *voiceless thing*. But the subject as such cannot be perceived or studied as if it were a thing, since it cannot remain a subject if it is voiceless; consequently, there is no knowledge of the subject but *dialogical* (40:363).

Such an insistence on the "person" must not be taken for a defense of psychological individualism; we shall see that nothing could be further from Bakhtin's thought. It is rather a question of insisting upon the singular, nonrepeatable nature of the facts that form the object of the human sciences.

Personalization is in no sense subjective. The boundary there is not the *I*, but this *I* in interrelation with other persons, that is *I* and the *other*, *I* and *Thou* (40: 370).

This personalism is semantic and not psychological (40:373).

Here, as elsewhere, one may be suprised by the absence of the word "historical": the term does not appear to have been thematized by Bakhtin, whereas the notion it covers (history) is actually basic for him.

The human sciences, and literary studies especially, suffer from an inferiority complex with respect to the natural sciences, and they would like to follow the latter's lead; but to do so is to sacrifice their specificity, forgetting that their "object" is precisely not an object but another subject. This fascination with "real" science can take several forms. Already in his earliest writings, Bakhtin shows that we tend to substitute for the real object of the human sciences (or literary studies) a reality that is purported to be more immediate, more tangible than their own. Two types of empirical objects are available for this enterprise: the text can be reduced to its materiality (a form of objective empiricism), or it can be dissolved into the psychic states (those that precede it and that follow it) felt by those who produce or perceive such a text (subjective empiricism).

The scholar latches on these two aspects, afraid of going beyond them in any way, habitually convinced that only metaphysical or mystical substances are to be found beyond. But such attempts to treat purely empirically the aesthetic object have always failed, and, as we have shown, are methodologically altogether illegitimate. . . . There is no reason to be afraid of the fact that the aesthetic object cannot be found in either psychical phenomena or in the material work; in no manner does it then become a mystical or metaphysical substance. The proteiform world of action, of ethical existence, is in the same situation. Where is the State? in the psyche? in physico-mathematical space? on the paper of constitutional documents? Where is the law? Nonetheless, we have a relationship to the State and to law, which we fully assume; more even: these values give meaning and order to empirical material as well as to our psyche, by allowing us to overcome its pure subjectivity (4:53).

In literary studies, both modes of empiricism are to be found among the Formalists. On the one hand, they commit the sin of *objective* empiricism when they want to reduce the work to its linguistic structures, and reduce the latter, if possible, to phonic material. Or else, they abandon all inquiry into intentions since these are not subject to direct observation. Bakhtin will oppose his own attitude to that of the Formalists:

We constantly insist upon the objectal and semantic aspects as well as upon the expressive, that is the intentional, since those are the forces that stratify and differentiate the common literary language, and we do so rather than pursue the linguistic markers (lexical colorations, semantic harmonies, etc.) of the languages of genres or of professional jargons, etc., markers which are, so to speak, the ossified deposits of the intentional process, and the signs of an interpretation of common linguistic forms abandoned along the way by the living labor of intention. These external markers, observable and identifiable on the linguistic level, must, in order to be apprehended, first be understood by means of an interpretation that follows the intention which animates them (21:105).

The requirement that language be apprehended not only in the forms produced but also through the productive forces (Humboldt's formulation: *energeia*, not *ergon*) finds its correlate on the recipient's side of the process, in insistent use of the notion of *horizon*.

It is necessary to emphasize once again that by "social language" we mean not the set of linguistic markers that determine the dialectological formation and differentiation of any given language, but the concrete and living set of the markers of such a social differentiation, which may occur just as easily within the framework of a linguistically homogeneous language, and be defined only by semantic displacements and lexical choices. It is a concrete sociolinguistic horizon that differentiates itself within the boundaries of an abstractly unified language. Frequently, this verbal horizon does not permit a rigorous linguistic definition, but it is pregnant with the possibility of eventually constituting itself into an autonomous dialect: it is a potential dialect, the embryo of a dialect not yet formed (21:168).

Objective empiricism is thus one of the figures of Formalism in literary studies; the other is *subjective* empiricism, particularly visible in such concepts as "habituation," "sensible" or "palpable" form, "defamiliarization" (*ostranenie*).

The foundations of their theory (to escape habituation, to make construction visible, etc.) definitely presuppose a subjective consciousness that "feels" (10:200). To assert that the work seeks to be "felt" is to practice the worst kind of psychologism, because the psycho-physiological process becomes then entirely self-sufficient and devoid of content, that is of any attachment to objective reality. Neither habituation nor perceptibility are objective features of the work, they are not within the work or its structure. The Formalists deride those who look for the "soul" or the "temper" in a literary work, but they themselves look in it for a psycho-physiological capability to produce stimulations (10:202).

It should not be too surprising that both forms of empiricism are to be found together among the Formalists: they have a common point of departure, which is the (Aristotelian) idea that it is possible, or even necessary, to conduct the study of the work independently of any idea that considers the participants in the communicative act that is literature (the author and the reader). But to proceed along this line is to study merely a part of a process that is understandable in its totality only.

In summary, these two points of view share the same defect: *they try to find the whole in the part*; they represent as the structure of the whole the structure of the part, which they isolate abstractly. Actually, the "artistic," in its totality, does not reside in the thing, or in the psyche of the creator, considered independently, not even in that of the contemplator: the artistic includes all three together. It is a *specific form of the relation between creator and contemplators, fixed in the artistic work* (7:248).

It is still a variant of objectivism, albeit a more abstract one, that is at work, according to Bakhtin, in the more recent structural studies.

In Structuralism, there is but one subject: the scholar himself. Things are changed into *notions* (of variable abstraction); but the subject can never become a notion (he speaks and answers for himself). Meaning is personal: there is always within it a question, an appeal to, and an anticipation of, the answer; there are always two subjects in it (the dialogical minimum) (40:372-3).

Another note elaborates his differences with Structuralists:

My relation to Structuralism. Against shutting oneself in the text. . . . The resulting formalization and depersonalization: all relations are of a logical nature (in the broad sense of the term). I, on the other hand, hear *voices* everywhere, and dialogical relations among them (40:372).

The strictures drawn against structural studies are thus part of a larger quarrel between subjectivists and objectivists (cf. Kierkegaard criticizing Hegel: "the subject can never become a notion.") Bakhtin defends subjectivity, but not that of the knowing person, as is usually the case, but that of the "thing" to be known. Or, as he puts it in one of the notes dating from the last years of his life:

The sciences of the spirit: their object is not one but two "spirits" (the studying

one and the studied, which must not fuse into a single one). Their true object is
the interrelation and interaction of the spirits (38:349).

Difference of Method

It will be no surprise that to such a radical difference in the object
there should correspond a difference of method; Bakhtin prefers, in
fact, to speak of *understanding* with respect to the human sciences
rather than knowledge, thus faithfully following the tradition of
Dilthey, Rickert, and Max Weber. Already in the writings of his youth,
on the occasion of an attack against the aesthetics and epistemology
of empathy (*Einfühlung*), Bakhtin describes understanding as a trans-
position that keeps nonfused two autonomous consciousnesses.

In its naive and realistic interpretation, the word "understanding" always induces
into error. It is not at all a question of an exact and passive reflexion, of a redoubling of the other's experience within me (such a redoubling is, in any case,
impossible), but a matter of translating the experience into an altogether different axiological perspective, into new categories of evaluation and formation
(3:91).

In subsequent writings, he will particularly stress the irreducible
duality of utterer and receiver. The first characteristic feature of understanding is that it tends to take the form of a reply elicited by the
initial remark (the object to be known).

All true understanding is active and already represents the embryo of an answer.
Only active understanding can apprehend the theme [the meaning of the utter-
ance]; it is only by means of becoming that becoming can be apprehended. . . .
All understanding is dialogical. Understanding is opposed to utterance like one
reply is opposed to another within a dialogue. Understanding is in search of a
counter-discourse to the discourse of the utterer (12:122-3).

There is no difference of nature here between the knowing discourse and the discourse to be known: they are cosubstantial, something that is obviously not the case as far as the natural sciences are
concerned.

Thoughts upon thoughts, experiences of experiences, discourse upon discourses,
texts bearing upon texts. Therein lies the fundamental particularity of our
(humanistic) disciplines by opposition to the natural sciences, although there,
too, there are no absolute or impenetrable boundaries (30:281).

Logically, one can certainly distinguish between language and
metalanguage, text and metatext, but, for Bakhtin, the metatextual

relation is not specific; the metatext is actually an intertext; the utterance that describes another utterance enters into a dialogical relation with it.

The shorthand record of the human sciences. It is always the record of a dialogue of a particular kind: the complex correlation of the *text* (object of study and reflexion) and the *context* that frames it and which is being created (as questions, objection, etc. are raised), where the scholar's knowing and evaluating thought accomplishes itself. It is the encounter of two texts: the already given text and the reacting text being created, and therefore, it is the encounter of two subjects, of two authors (30:285).

Understanding as a setting in relation with other texts and as reinterpretation in a new context (mine, that of my epoch, the future's). . . . True understanding in literature and in literary studies is always historical and personal. . . . *Things pregnant with words* (40:364-365). Is there a counterpart to "context" in the natural sciences? [No.] Context is always personal (an infinite dialogue without first or last word), whereas the natural sciences deal with an objective system (devoid of subjects) (40:370).

Or more briefly: "Metalanguage isn't just a code: it is always in a dialogical relation to the language it describes and analyzes" (38:340).

Because of this fundamental difference, the very terms of "science," "knowledge," etc., do not have the same meaning as they are applied in one area or the other.

The interpretation of symbolic structures is forced to go deep into the infinity of symbolic meanings; that is why it cannot become scientific, in the sense of the term in the *exact* sciences. The interpretation of meanings cannot be scientific, but it is profoundly cognitive (40:362).

Bakhtin is not content with this negative observation; he proposes to introduce two different terms to describe the ideal sought in each case (these ideals are not identical, and the inferiority complex of the human sciences vis-à-vis the natural sciences is groundless). For the natural sciences, accuracy counts above all.

Accuracy presupposes the coincidence of the thing with itself (28:410). The limit of accuracy in the natural sciences is identification (a=a) (40:371).

For the human sciences, on the other hand, it is depth that is essential.

There the knowing subject does not question itself nor a third party standing in front of the dead thing; it puts the question to the knowable itself. The criterion is not the accuracy of knowledge but the depth of the insight (28:409). The object of the human sciences is *expressive* and *speaking being*. Such a being never coincides with itself, that is why it is inexhaustible in its meaning and signification (28:410). The importance of the stake in gaining access to the creative kernel of the person, ever more deeply (in the creative kernel, the person continues to live, s/he remains immortal). . . . In the human sciences, accuracy consists in overcoming the other's strangeness without assimilating it wholly to oneself (all sorts of substitutions, modernizations, non-recognitions of the stranger, etc.) (40:371).

Linguistics and Translinguistics

The text is the common object of all human sciences, yet human sciences are several, and are not reducible to only one from among themselves. The epistemology of science rightly asserts that a science is not determined by a real object but by an object-to-be-known, which arises in the adoption of a different perspective with respect to the very same object.

From the indication of the real object we must pass to a precise settling of the boundaries of the objects of scientific research. The real object is social man speaking and expressing himself through other means (30:292).

Language, discourse, that is almost the totality of human life. But it must not be thought that this totalizing and multifaceted reality can be the object of a single science—linguistics, and thus be understood through linguistic methods exclusively (30:297).

Among all the perspectives possible for the consideration of this unique object, two receive Bakhtin's attention: one is linguistics; the other is a discipline that, initially, has no name (unless it be sociology), but he will come to call it, in his last writings, *metalingvistika*, a term which I will translate by *translinguistics*, to avoid possible confusion. The term in current usage that would correspond best to Bakhtin's aim probably is *pragmatics*, and one could say without exaggeration that Bakhtin is the modern founder of this discipline.

Linguistics and translinguistics represent two different points of view on the same object, language. In his early thinking, Bakhtin does not see things quite as neutrally, but rather tends to say, especially in *Marxism and the Philosophy of Language* (a work signed Voloshinov), that translinguistics (yet to come) must supplant linguistics, because one of the objects of knowledge is more real, or more important, or more legitimate than the other. But, in other texts, some of which are written contemporaneously with this book, he insists, on the contrary, on the legitimacy of both perspectives.

In its construction of the notion of language and that of its elements—syntactical, morphological, lexical, and others, linguistics brackets away the forms of organization of concrete utterances and their social and ideological functions. . . . Such a bracketing away is perfectly legitimate, necessary, and required by the cognitive and practical objectives of linguistics itself. Without it, the notion of language as system could not be constructed (10:117).

Language as the specific object of linguistics, obtained by the bracketing away, perfectly legitimate and necessary, of some aspects of the concrete life of discourse . . . ; some aspects of the life of discourse that exceed, in perfectly legitimate fashion, the frame of linguistics (32:242).

One may well wonder if this desire to assure the others of the "legitimate" character of their position does not proceed in fact from the reciprocal desire to have the others, namely the linguists, recognize for their part the fact that Bakhtin's own position is "perfectly necessary."

From this distinction emerges a consequence of considerable importance, glimpsed by Bakhtin in his earliest writings: the impossibility of patterning a science of discourse (such as poetics) on a science of language (linguistics).

In perfectly uncritical manner, the Formalists project the constructive particularities of poetical works into the system of language, just as they transpose directly linguistic elements into poetic construction. This leads, whether openly or surreptitiously, to the wrong orientation of poetics toward linguistics in greater or lesser measure. . . . Such attempts are based upon the entirely unproven presupposition that the linguistic element of the tongue and the constructive element of the work must necessarily coincide. We assume that they do not, and cannot, coincide, since the two phenomena belong to different planes (10:118-19).

To begin with, the object of linguistics is constituted by *language* and its subdivisions (phonemes, morphemes, propositions, etc.) whereas that of translinguistics is *discourse*, which is represented in turn by individual *utterances*. To name the latter, Bakhtin has recourse to a Russian word that can have several distinct meanings: *slovo*, which somewhat like Greek *logos*, means both "word" and "discourse" (among other things). And it is obvious that when the term is used to describe the object of translinguistics, it is equivalent to "discourse."

Discourse, that is language in its concrete and living totality (32:242); *discourse*, that is language as a concrete total phenomenon (32:244); *discourse*, that is utterance (*vyskazyvanie*) (32:246).

We will see later in detail what are the specific features of the utterance; but it is already clear that the utterance is the product of a working up, in which linguistic matter is but one of the ingredients; another is all that is brought to a verbal production by the fact of it being uttered, that is its unique historical, social, cultural, context. The decisive role of the context of the uttering in the determination of the overall meaning of the utterance, and the fact that this context is, by definition, unique (if only at the temporal level), leads to the opposition of the units of language to the instances of discourse, that is to utterances, along the line of the *reiterative* versus the *unique*.

The utterance (the verbal work) as nonreiterative whole, historically unique and individual. . . . The entities of language studied by linguistics are by definition reproducible in an unlimited number of utterances (as are equally reproducible the models of propositions). It is true that the frequency of repetition is different for different entities (maximal for phonemes, minimal for sentences). It is in fact through this reproducibility alone, that they can be entities of language and assume their function. . . . The entities of verbal communication—whole utterances—are non-reproducible (although they can be quoted) and are bound among themselves by dialogic relations (30:307).

I can certainly repeat the sentence that I have just uttered, but in spite of all apparent identities, the two utterances will not be identical: the status of the second is nearer to that of citation.

This difference between language and discourse determines very exactly the paradox of translation.

Every system of signs (that is, every "language"), no matter how limited the collectivity that adopts it by convention, can always be, in principle, deciphered, that is translated into other sign systems (other languages); therefore, there exists a general logic of sign systems, a language of languages, potential and unified (obviously it can never become a particular concrete language, a language among others). But a text (as distinct from language as a system of means) can never be fully translated, because there is no text of texts, potential and unified (30:284-85).

The disclosure of the nonreiterative nature of textual facts brings us back to the issues of general epistemology we started out with. Bakhtin begins by wondering whether the uniqueness he has uncovered pertains solely to the object of the human sciences or whether it is to be found in natural objects as well: what could be more unique, for example, than a fingerprint? Moreover, in both instances, a mechanical reproduction is always possible (a book exists in many copies; a fingerprint can be duplicated ad infinitum). Such a reasoning holds, however, only if the text is reduced to a material object, that is, if it is already treated like the objects of natural sciences. It becomes necessary for Bakhtin then to further elaborate the (impossible) nature of the reproduction he has in mind with respect to texts: it implies the intervention of a subject (which must not be thought of in terms of individuals, as we shall see).

Natural uniqueness (the fingerprint, for example) and the signifying (semiotic) nonreiterativity of the text. Only a mechanical reproduction for the fingerprint (in unlimited quantity); such a mechanical reproduction is, of course, also possible for the text (a reprinting, for example); but the reproduction of a text by a *subject* (return to the text, new reading, new performance, citation) is a new and nonreiterative event in the life of the text, a new link in the historical chain of verbal communication (30:284).

A new epistemological difficulty arises then. If utterances are unique, can they still constitute the objects of a science? It will be recalled that this argument led Saussure to exclude speech (*parole*) from the object of linguistics. Bakhtin will explicitly oppose this manner of approaching the issue by asserting, as we shall see, that the domain of speech belongs to the social order, and not merely to the individual. How then to overcome this difficulty? Bakhtin makes an attempt in one of his very last texts.

The question arises whether science can deal with individual entities of absolutely nonreiterative nature such as utterances, or whether these do not fall beyond the scope of generalizing scientific knowledge. Of course it can. First of all, the points of departure of every science are nonreiterative unique entities, and the science in question remains attached to them all along its course. Second, science, and especially philosophy, can and must study the specific form and function of such unique entities (30:287).

This answer may leave us bemused, not because it seems inappropriate, but because it appears to simply annul the distinctions worked out previously. The two justifications Bakhtin advances apply equally to all sciences and preserve nothing of the specificity of utterances: not only linguistics, he appears to claim, but the natural sciences as well deal continually with individual fact; the only question is to know its place. And translinguistics sheds it special status since it studies, in turn, the general aspects (the forms and functions) of the peculiar beings that are utterances. Must we conclude then that Bakhtin's previous reflections were groundless?

It may be possible to go beyond this aporia if we accept a dissociation of two oppositions that seem to be confused in Bakhtin, who, in this respect, remains faithful to Dilthey's teachings. If utterances are considered in their specificity and uniqueness, they become the objects of history (literary history in the case of works) and not of translinguistics. The latter does not study each utterance as to what makes it unique, but as to the laws of its functioning, as indeed is the case in Bakhtin's own work in translinguistics. The same is true of the other human sciences: general sociology or anthropology are not to be confused with history or ethnography, no more than psychology can be reduced to the study of particular cases, whether pathological or not. The difference lies, in each instance, between the general theory of an object and the interpretation of the particular instances that constitute it. By no means can this signify that translinguistics is confused with linguistics, since the objects of knowledge in each of these perspectives remain distinct. Yet it is this confusion that appears to explain the absence, in Bakhtin, of a theorization of the relation between translinguistics and (literary) history. Even less can one assimilate human and natural sciences, and abandon Bakhtin's contribution in the matter: the distinction does rest, as he states, on the difference of nature of the objects of knowledge (or upon the absence of "object" in the human sciences). But this does not allow us to grant, in Dilthey's fashion, all theorizing exclusively to the natural sciences, and to reserve the sole use of interpretation to the human sciences; here as well as there, both must necesssarily be practiced.

Chapter Three
Major Options

The Individual and the Social

At the end of the twenties, three books were published by Bakhtin's circle; they deal respectively with psychology, linguistics, and literary studies; all three are written in polemical style, and present themselves as Marxist. The opposition at stake in these polemics, as indeed in other writings from this period, is that of the social versus the individual, the latter term designating the schools or currents of thought under attack, while the former is claimed as the necessary point of departure for Marxist psychology, linguistics, or literary studies.

Pyschology is the object of Voloshinov/Bakhtin's book *Freudianism* (1927). In the early pages, the author adumbrates contemporary tendencies in psychology, finally grouping them into "subjective" and "objective" psychology; the first, which is the target of the polemic, is represented most notably by psychoanalysis. The critique of Freudianism is based on the postulate recalled in the preceding chapter: language is constitutive of human existence. Yet—and that is the first important assertion in *Freudianism*—language is also thoroughly social.

There is nothing obvious about this assertion. It could in fact be objected that the act of sound production or perception is purely individual, and physiological, and that no sociality need be presupposed. This is granted readily by Voloshinov/Bakhtin, but only to add that these two acts are nothing without a third: the production and reception of meaning. It is this act that truly founds language.

*The "signification" of discourse and the "understanding" of this signification by
the other (or by others) . . . . exceed the boundaries of the isolated physiological organisms* and presuppose *the interaction of several organisms,* which implies
that this third component of verbal reaction has a *sociological character* (8:31).

Meaning (communication) implies community. Concretely, one always addresses someone, and that someone does not assume a purely
passive role (as the term "recipient" could lead one to infer): the
interlocutor participates in the formation of the meaning of the utterance, just as the other elements—similarly social—of the context
of uttering do.

No utterance in general can be attributed to the speaker exclusively; it is the
product of the interaction of the interlocutors, and, broadly speaking, the product of the whole complex *social situation* in which it has occurred (8:118).[1]

It is not necessary then to be actually addressing someone else:
even the most personal act, becoming conscious of oneself, always
already implies an interlocutor, the other's glance upon us.

The entire verbal part of human existence (external and internal discourse) cannot be charged to the account of the unique subject, taken in isolation; it does
not belong to the individual but to his *social group* (his social environment).
. . . . The motivation of our action, the attainment of self-consciousness (and
self-consciousness is always verbal; it always leads to the search for a specific
verbal complex), is always a way of putting oneself in relation to a given social
norm; it is, so to speak, a socialization of the self and of its action. Becoming
conscious of myself, I attempt to see myself through the eyes of another person,
of another representative of my social group or of my class (8:128-30).

It will be noted that, for Bakhtin, "society" begins with the appearance of the second person. Although it claims to be Marxist, his
conception of sociability seems to be slightly heterodox: it consists,
in a way, in considering intersubjectivity as logically preceding subjectivity.
If language is constitutively intersubjective (social), and if it is
also essential to human existence, then the conclusion is inescap-
able: human existence is originally social, and cannot be reduced to
its biological dimension without being deprived of those characteristics that make it human; hence, Voloshinov/Bakhtin's opposition to
any biological or subjective (individualistic) psychology.

There is no such thing as abstract biological personality, this biological individual
that has become the alpha and the omega of contemporary ideology. There is no
human being outside society, and therefore not outside objective socioeconomic

conditions. That is a case of bad abstraction. *Human personality becomes historically real and culturally productive only insofar as it is part of a social whole, in its class and through its class.* To enter into history, it is not enough to be born physically—that is the way of animals, yet they do not enter history. A second birth, *social* this time, is necessary as it were. A human being is not born in the guise of an abstract biological organism, but as a landowner or a peasant, a bourgeois or a proletarian, and that is of the essence. Then, he is born Russian or French, and finally he is born in 1800 or in 1900. Only such a social and historical localization makes man real, and determines the content of his personal and cultural creation (8:23-4). The content of psychic life is thoroughly ideological: from the vague thought and indeterminate and confused decor, all the way to the philosophical system or even the complex political institution, we have at our disposal a continuous series of ideological, and therefore sociological, phenomena (8:37).[2]

This is the general conception from which Voloshinov/Bakhtin will launch his critiques of Freudianism. As he sees it, Freudianism ultimately grounds human psychic life on a biological base, and conceives of the unconscious as preceding, or external to, language. Yet, the only access we have to it is mediated by language (the patient's discourse), and nothing permits us to see it as a territory free of any verbal trace.

The motifs of the unconscious revealed during psychoanalytic sessions by means of the method of "free association" are *verbal reactions* of the patient, as are all the other habitual motifs of consciousness. They are different one from the other, so to speak, not by any generic distinction of their being, but only by their content, that is *ideologically*. In this sense, the unconscious according to Freud can be defined as an "unauthorized consciousness" in distinction to the habitual "official" consciousness (8:127-28).

In their analyses, Freud and his disciples always tend to play up individual motivations (aggressivity toward the father, attraction for the mother, etc.), but aren't the words of the patient, uttered during the analytic session, determined as well, if not more, by the interaction that comes into being in the microsociety formed by the physician and the patient (given the role of the interlocutor, which is now familiar to us)?

What is reflected in these verbal utterances is not the dynamics of the individual soul, but the *social dynamics* of the interrelations of doctor and patient (8:119).

Voloshinov/Bakhtin would even say that it is not the relation patient-physician that results from transference, for example of an

Oedipal relation to the father, but rather that the reverse occurs: memories are interpreted in the light of the structure of the present situation.

Would it not be more correct to say that the physician and the patient, having joined forces, are doing nothing but projecting into the unconscious complex (paternal or maternal) their present relations, inherent to the treatment (more precisely, some aspects of them, or their general schema, since these relations are very complex)? (6:204)

Thereafter, Voloshinov/Bakhtin's general attitude will not be to reject the facts observed by Freud, but to reinterpret them in a framework governed by the idea that man is a verbal, and therefore social, animal.

The strength of Freud lies in having brought these questions to light, and to have gathered materials for their examination. His weakness is to have failed to understand the sociological essence of all of these phenomena and to have attempted to insert them into the narrow limits of the individual organism and its psychic life. He explains processes that are essentially social from the perspective of a purely individual psychology (8:36).

The vaguest thought, left unspoken, just as much as a complex philosophical development, presupposes organized communication among individuals (admittedly, different forms and degrees of organization of this communication). Whereas Freud derives the entire ideological series, from the first to its last component, from the simplest elements of individual psychic life, as if we existed in a social void (8:38).

And what if the difference between the conscious and the unconscious were no more than a difference between two models of discourse? The difference between the Ego and the Super-Ego, that which exists between a sender and an imaginary receiver that has been interiorized?

The parts of quotidian ideology [zhitejskaja, a concept introduced by Voloshinov/ Bakhtin in opposition to explicit "official ideology"], which correspond to the conscious according to Freud (official, censored consciousness), express the more stable and dominant aspects of class consciousness. . . . In these layers of quotidian ideology, internal discourse is easily ordered, and it readily turns into external discourse. . . . Other layers—those corresponding to the Freudian unconscious—are far removed from the stable system of dominant ideology. . . . The more clear-cut and the deeper the break between official and unofficial consciousness, the more difficult it is for the motifs of internal discourse to pass into external discourse (8:133-34).

Bakhtin does not return explicitly to these questions in his later writings, but he does not fail to evidence, in passing, his familiarity with Freudian concepts, and to point up that his judgment had not varied: he continues to consider language as logically preceding the unconscious.

The attempt to understand the interaction with the discourse of the other by means of psychoanalysis and the "collective unconscious." What psychologists (and especially psychiatrists) reveal existed in the past; it is preserved, but not in the unconscious, not even a collective one, but in the memory of languages, genres, rituals; that is where it comes from to enter into people's discourses and dreams (narrated, consciously remembered) (38:349).

We shall see that Bakhtin's own psychological ideas derive from Dostoevsky and not Freud, and that, in his view, the two are incompatible. A sentence evokes this opposition indirectly: "Consciousness is far more frightening than all unconscious complexes" (31:313). That is because, for Bakhtin, "at the bottom of man" we find not the Id but the other.

Marxism and the Philosophy of Language is published two years after *Freudianism*; it is also signed Voloshinov, and devotes its first half to a parallel critique of contemporary linguistics. Here again, the various tendencies within the field are classed into two groups, but this time both are condemned. On the one hand, we have a linguistics of classical inspiration, or "abstract objectivism" as it will be called, which extends from general grammars to Saussure and Bally: this form of linguistics wants to know only the abstract form of the language and casts out speech (parole) from its object of inquiry, alleging that it is individual and therefore infinitely variable. On the other hand, we have Romantic linguistics, or "individualistic subjectivism," from Humboldt to Vossler and Spitzer, which grants recognition and value to individual variations, and refuses to take into account the fiction that is "language." Although they appear to be opposed, these two doctrines in fact share a decisive presupposition, namely that utterance is individual. Voloshinov/Bakhtin believes the opposite to be true.

Thus the speaking subject, taken from the inside, so to speak, turns out to be wholly the product of social interrelations. Not only external expression but also internal experience fall within social territory. Therefore, the road which links the internal experience (the "expressible") to its external objectification (the "utterance") lies entirely in social territory (12:107).

Both schools of linguistics are dismissed for their common failure to apprehend verbal reality.

The isolated utterance (parole), the doctrine of abstract objectivism notwithstanding, is nowise an individual fact that, as such, allegedly does not lend itself to sociological analysis. . . . But individualistic subjectivism *is wrong* in that it ignores and does not understand the social nature of the utterance, and in that it attempts to deduce it from the internal world of the speaker as the expression of this internal world. The structure of the utterance, just like that of expressible experience, is a *social structure* (12:11112).

Finally, the same postulates and the same critiques are to be found in the field of literary studies. The polemical analysis of Formalism, *The Formal Method in Literary Studies* (1928), signed Medvedev, is subtitled: "Critical Introduction to Sociological Poetics" (my emphasis); and, in the preface of the first book to appear under his name, *Problems of Dostoevsky's Work* (1929), Bakhtin writes:

At the bottom of this analysis is to be found the conviction that every literary work is sociological, and that it is so internally, immanently (13:3).

When, several years later, Bakhtin turns to stylistics, he begins with the same critical observation (it is true that this stylistics is attached to principles advanced by Vossler).

Stylistics . . . does not know how to discern, beyond the mutations of individuals or currents, the great anonymous destinies of literary discourse. In most instances, stylistics is concerned only with chamber art, and it slights the social life of discourse beyond the artist's studio, in the vast spaces of public squares, streets, cities and villages, social groups, generations, and epochs (21:73).

No attempt will be made to follow up these theses concerning the predominance of the social on the individual, with an explanation of the effect of singularity that a work (or an individual) can produce. Bakhtin's books on specific authors—Rabelais, Dostoevsky—actually raise questions of genre, epochs, or general theory, and not individuals. Bakhtin will remain faithful to this option all his life.

Form and Content

A second dichotomy always present in Bakhtin's writings, especially in the twenties but continuing to the end of his trajectory, is that of form and content. In this instance, however, and in distinction to the opposition of the individual and the social, he does not valorize one of the terms to better condemn the other; rather, he asserts the

necessity of finding a link between the two, of taking both into account simultaneously, and of maintaining a perfect balance between
them. In the preface to *Problems of Dostoevsky's Work* (1929),
Bakhtin indicates that his objective is to go beyond "narrow" ideologism" as well as "narrow formalism"; he uses almost the same phrase
in the preamble to "Discourse in the Novel."

The guiding idea of this work is that the study of verbal art can and must overcome the breach between an abstract "formal" approach and an equally abstract
"ideological" approach (21:72).

The same will to synthesize is still present in the later writings. For
example, in introducing the category of the chronotope, he asserts:
"We understand the chronotope as a literary category of form-and-
content [*formal'no-soderzhatel'nuju*]" (23:235). And qualifying
Dostoevsky's contribution to the history of the novel:

These discoveries have a form-and-content character. Their *formal* content is
deeper, denser, more general than the concrete and changing ideological content
that fills them in Dostoevsky (31:309).

When Bakhtin adopts a critical stance in this matter, it is not
against form or against content (as he was "against" the individual),
but against those who isolate the study of one or the other: the pure
ideologists and the pure formalists. Among the first, the most common error consists in extracting an element of the work, say a statement or a character, and to confront it directly with its counterpart
in social life, without taking into account the relations established
between this element and the other components of the work, whereas it is these relations that in fact determine alone its meaning.

For the Marxist, direct conclusions, drawn from the secondary reflection of an
ideology in literature, and projected on the social reality of the corresponding
epoch, are totally inadmissible; that was, and continues to be, the practice of
the pseudo-sociologists, who are ready to project any structural element of the
literary work—a character, or the plot, for example, directly upon real life. For
the true sociologist, the hero of the novel or the event in the plot are of course
far more revealing precisely because they are elements of the artistic structure,
that is they are in relation to their own artistic relation and taken for direct and
naive projections upon life (10:32-33).

Just as the character can be understood only in relation to the
work, so the work must first be put in relation to the whole of literature. The latter is not in fact in direct communication with the world
of socioeconomic realities: it needs the mediation of ideology. This

series of relays, whose counterpart can be found in nearly identical form in "Literary Evolution" by Tynianov, dating from the same period, cannot be ignored unless one wants to lock oneself into primary sociologism.

The work cannot be understood outside the entity in "literature." But this latter entity, taken as a whole, as well as its elements—and therefore the work in question—cannot be understood outside the entity "ideological life." This entity in turn cannot be studied, either in part or in whole, outside the unitary socioeconomic laws. . . . One cannot skip any of the links of the continuous chain constituted by the understanding of the ideological phenomenon, and one cannot stop at one link without going on to the next. It is perfectly inadmissable to study the literary work directly and exclusively as an element of the ideological milieu, as if it were the only instance of literature, whereas it is directly the element of the literary world in its specificity (10:41-42).

However, it is not against the partisans of the "content" only tendency that most of Bakhtin's critiques are addressed; rather it is against the Formalists. The reason is simple: in the years that preceded his entry into literary life, the Formalists held center stage. If Bakhtin came to occupy the position of "synthesis"—reconciling literature and the history of ideas—then the Formalists' position is that of the antithetic pole, since they criticize the holders of what would have to be the thesis, that is those who reduce literature to the history of ideas. They will become therefore his favorite target.

Bakhtin's relation to (Russian) Formalism is not simple; it blends participation and opposition. First, it should be noted that, in the critical writings that he devotes to it, in the twenties, Bakhtin always precedes or follows his strictures with a very positive general evaluation. For example, in his article "The Problem of Content, Material, and Form in Verbal Artistic Creation" (of 1924):

There is conducted in Russia presently in the field of knowledge of art, work of the highest seriousness and fruitfulness. These past few years, Russian scholarship has gained precious works on the theory of art, especially in the field of poetics (4:7).

Or in the book *The Formal Method in Literary Studies*:

On the whole, Formalism has played a fruitful role. It has brought to the forefront the essential problems of literary scholarship, and it has done so in such acute fashion that they cannot henceforth be evaded or ignored. Their very errors, the courage and the coherence of these errors, contribute so much the more to attract attention to the problems raised (10:232).

It is interesting to recall also another judgment, formulated in 1970, in answer to a question on the present state of literary studies.

We have great scholarly traditions, developed in the past (Potebnia and Veselovski) as well as during the Soviet period (Tynianov, Tomashevski, Eikhenbaum, Gukovski, and others) (36:328).

It is obviously significant that, of all literary studies carried out in the Soviet Union, Bakhtin cites only the works of three Formalists and of one of their disciples! It is possible, besides, that Bakhtin's strategic perspective had changed at this time: the Formalists had ceased playing, for a long time, any major role in the theoretical literary debates in Russia, and Bakhtin may have considered the moment opportune to underscore what linked him to them rather than what separated him. There is no reason, however, to think that he changed his mind on the substance of the question.

The main reproach he directs against them is already to be found in the 1924 study. It has two parts: the Formalists are wrong to isolate the study of literature from that of art in general, in other words, from aesthetics, and, ultimately, from philosophy; their positivistic refusal to examine their own foundations does not make them immune to aesthetics or philosophy; it merely leaves them in the shadows. Bakhtin will take it upon himself therefore to formulate their implicit ideology, which he identifies as an "aesthetics of the materials." For the Formalists, it is the materials (in literature: language) that wholly determine artistic forms. Such an approach, continues Bakhtin, necessarily leads to the valorization of empty and dead forms, to the separation of form and content. In this argument, Bakhtin closely follows Riegl's critique (in *Stilfragen*) of other contemporary authors, such as Semper (we shall see why this comparison is significant).

The book by Medvedev/Bakhtin amplifies this criticism. Numerous inconsistencies, obscurities, and shortcomings in Formalist doctrine are pointed out, and the nefarious consequences of maintaining the disjunction of form and content are made manifest. Without going into the details of this ancient polemic, one can say that Medvedev/Bakhtin's arguments clearly bore home and that they were convincing.

But this does not mean that the matter is therefore resolved. For the Formalist doctrine that is the butt of Bakhtin's attacks does not correspond exactly to the actual activities of the group. There is a genuine difference between the Formalists' declarations of principle that Bakhtin generally analyzes, and the ideas, sometimes implicit, that can be drawn from their concrete work: whereas the declarations are but a variant, influenced by linguistics, of Romantic aesthetics (notably through the notion of "poetic language"), the ideas suggested lead to the discovery of numberless aspects of the literary work that criticism had ignored until then; they also ultimately bring about a disavowal of the possibility of a linguistic definition of literature. The very objects of Bakhtin's study in the years to come were first delineated and brought to the attention of theoreticians in the works of the Formalists: for example, narrative voice by Eikhenbaum, or the dialogue of texts by Tynianov. It is only in his very last text that Bakhtin seems to acknowledge this dimension of the Formalists' work: "The positive signification of Formalism (new problems and new aspects of art)" (40:372).

But let us return to his reflection in those days. The criticism of the Russian Formalists is accompanied in *The Formal Method in Literary Studies* by an enthusiastic exposition of another doctrine, called by Bakhtin: "Western Formalism" (the term "Formalism" is actually no longer appropriate). This expression refers to the writings of a group of German-born art theorists (painting and sculpture) that included K. Fielder, A. Hildebrand, A. Riegl, W. Worringer, and H. Wölfflin. Bakhtin had been relatively critical toward them in his first book (1922-24); what Medvedev/Bakhtin appreciates now in the Western "Formalists" is precisely their refusal to lock themselves up in the exclusive study of either form or content, and their simultaneous struggle against positivism (formalism) and idealism (ideologism).

Essentially against idealism, and, more generally against all abstract ideologism in the interpretation of art, [Western] Formalism promoted the idea of the closed structural unity of the work; but then, against positivism, it stressed with all possible power the deep semantic saturation of every element of artistic structure. That is why this "Formalism" isn't really one. Nothing is more foreign to the European formal current than an underestimation of the semantic importance of all the elements, without exception, that constitute an artistic structure (10:68).

The chief concept put forward by the Western Formalists in their study of art is not "form" (or "art") but *architectonics*, a term introduced by Hildebrand; Medvedev/Bakhtin would like to replace it, while preserving its role, by *structure* or *construction* (*Konstrukcija*, a word equally important to Tynianov at the time). "It is the structure of the literary work that must be the object of poetics" (10:141).

That is why Medvedev/Bakhtin's overall judgment of Western "Formalism" is very positive (and we shall see that Bakhtin borrows some important elements from these theories.)

The formal current in art studies in the West exceeds any artistic program, and though artistic preferences are not altogether alien to it, but they vary among the authors, it is, in its fundamental intention, valid for all art. It establishes the specific features of art, as well as the constitutive traits of each form of art considered separately, and of each of the currents that can be distinguished (6:68).

The problems it raises and the fundamental tendencies it embraces in its solutions seem to us generally acceptable (10:76).

This does not mean that Medvedev/Bakhtin refrains from any criticism of the Western "Formalists": he takes them to task notably for their lack of sociohistorical perspective, as well as, in somewhat abstract (and perhaps hypocritical) fashion for their "philosophical ground" (10:76).

It is also in *The Formal Method in Literary Studies* that Medvedev/ Bakhtin attempts to make more explicit, though in general terms, the nature of his middle way, the approach to literary works that would allow equal consideration of form and content. Here is a formulation of the problem:

The problem raised would be resolved if one managed to find, in the poetical work, an element that would at once participate in the material presence of the discourse and in its signification, that would be the mediation between the depth and generality of its meaning and the singularity of its utterance. Such a mediation will create the possibility of a continuous passage from the periphery of the work to the kernel of its internal signification, from external form to internal ideological meaning (10:161-62).

And here are, in answer, the first attempts to resolve the problem:

What is, in reality, this element that unites the material presence of discourse with its meaning? We submit that this element is social evaluation [*ocenka*] (10:162). We call social evaluation the historical reality that unites the singular presence of the utterance to the generality and plenitude of its meaning, that embodies meaning in a unique and concrete situation, and gives, here and now, a signification to the sound presence of the discourse (10:164).

Between the generality of the meaning of words, such as we find them in the dictionary, and that of the rules of grammar, and, on the other hand, the uniqueness of the acoustic event that occurs when an utterance is proffered, there takes place a process that permits the linkage of the two, which we call *enunciation*. This process does not suppose the simple existence of two physical bodies, those of the sender and the receiver, but the presence of two (or more) social entities, that translate the *voice* of the sender and the *horizon* of the receiver. The time and the space in which enunciation occurs also aren't purely physical categories, but a historical time and a social space. Human intersubjectivity is actualized through particular utterances.

Every element of the work can be compared to a thread joining human beings. The work as a whole is the set of these threads, that creates a complex, differentiated, social interaction, between the persons who are in contact with it (10:205).

In this book, we remain at a level of generality. But as early as the following year, Bakhtin published, under his own name, his first studies of specific works, those of Dostoevsky and Tolstoy (especially the "Preface" to *Resurrection*); these seem to represent an implementation of the principles formulated earlier, since it is by means of the determination of voices and horizons, and therefore of the conceptions of the world that are expressed in them, that the analysis proceeds. The writings of the thirties, and especially those upon the chronotope, will reinforce and complete this approach, that intends to neglect neither form nor content.

It would be legitimate then to grant to Bakhtin the position to which he aspires, namely that of the synthesis that comes after the ideologist "thesis" and the Formalist "antithesis." It is in this sense that he is "post-Formalist": he exceeds Formalism, but only after having absorbed its teachings. It is certainly not by chance if the great works of criticism produced since, which one would think of comparing with the work of Bakhtin, proceed from a similar movement of going beyond, but also absorbing, previous formalist schools; for example, Auerbach's *Mimesis*, which puts the "new stylistics" (of Spitzer's vintage) in the service of a historical and social vision, or Ian Watt's *The Rise of the Novel*, which leaves I. A. Richard's semantics to build a literary history that would be in relation to the history of ideas and to social history. The simple rejection of, or the pure ignorance of, Formalism, on the other hand, have never led to any kind of movement "beyond."

Chapter Four
Theory of the Utterance

First Formulations

Bakhtin formulates his theory of the utterance twice: in the texts of the late twenties, signed almost exclusively by Voloshinov, and then, some thirty years later, in some writings from the late fifties. I shall present these two syntheses separately, though the differences between them are not major.

The first formulations attempting to define a theory of the utterance are to be found in one of Voloshinov/Bakhtin's oldest articles: "Discourse in Life and Discourse in Poetry" (1926). It starts with an observation: linguistic matter constitutes only a part of the utterance; there exists another part that is nonverbal, which corresponds to the context of the enunciation. The existence of such a context has not been unknown before Bakhtin, but it had always been looked upon as external to the utterance, whereas Bakhtin asserts that it is an integral part of it.

In no instance is the extraverbal situation only an external cause of the utterance; it does not work from the outside like a mechanical force. On the contrary, the situation enters into the utterance as a necessary constitutive element of its semantic structure. The quotidian [zhiznennoe] utterance endowed with signification is therefore composed of two parts: (1) a realized or actualized verbal part, and (2) an implied part. That is why an utterance can be compared to an "enthymeme" (7:251).

41

What does the context of enunciation consist in? To find the answer, Voloshinov/Bakhtin imagines a minimal utterance of the kind: "So!" or "Hm . . . yes!" and puts side by side our perplexity in the face of the verbal part alone and the interpretation we easily come up with when we know the context in which the utterance was made. By a kind of subtraction, he arrives at the following elements:

The extraverbal context of the utterance is composed of three aspects: (1) The spatial *horizon common* to the interlocutors (the unity of the visible: the room, the window, etc.); (2) *Knowledge and understanding of the situation*, also *common* to both; (3) Their *common evaluation* of the situation (7:250).

The implicit part of the utterance is nothing more than the interlocutors' common horizon of spatiotemporal, semantic, and evaluative (axiological) elements.

Common to the interlocutors: this feature—essential in Voloshinov/Bakhtin's perspective—must be emphasized, for, he insists, it must not be taken as what *I* know, *I* want, *I* see, or *I* love:

Only that which *we*, the set of interlocutors, know, see, love, and recognize— only that in which *we* are all united—can become the implied part of the utterance. . . . "I" can actualize itself in discourse only by relying upon "we." In this way every quotidian utterance appears as an objective and social enthymeme. It is like a "password" known only to those who belong to the same social horizon (7:251).

A few years later, Voloshinov/Bakhtin proposes a slightly different description of the context of enunciation: he keeps the third characteristic feature (collective evaluation) but drops the second (shared knowledge); the first (the common horizon), however, is analyzed in two aspects, spatiotemporal coordinates and object (referent).

Let us agree to use the familiar word *situation* for the three implied aspects of the extraverbal part of the utterance: the *space* and *time* of the enunciation ("where" and "when"), the object or *theme* of the utterance (that "of which" it is spoken); and the *relation* of the interlocutors to what is happening ("evaluation") (18:76).

We can understand better now why Voloshinov/Bakhtin had to begin not only with a critique of the Saussurean school, for whom the utterance, as individual, was not relevant, but also of the "individualistic subjectivism" school (Vossler and his disciples): although better than the Saussureans in that it does not dismiss the utterance, it is nonetheless wrong to believe it is individual.

Whatever the moment of the utterance-expression we may consider, it will always be determined by the real conditions of its uttering, and foremost by the *nearest social situation* (12:101).

Verbal communication will never be understood or explained outside of this link to the concrete situation (12:114).

In other words, the difference between the utterance and the proposition (or the sentence)—a unit of language—consists in that the first is necessarily produced in a particular context that is always social, whereas the second does not need a context. Sociability has a dual origin: first, the utterance is addressed to someone (which means that we have at the very least the microsociety formed by two persons, the speaker and the receiver); second, the speaker is always already a social being.

Voloshinov/Bakhtin is especially attached to the first part of this assertion; it recurs repeatedly in the writings published at the end of the twenties: the utterance is not the business of the speaker alone, but the result of his or her interaction with a listener, whose reactions he or she integrates in advance.

The utterance is constructed between two socially organized persons, and, should there not be present an actual interlocutor, one is presupposed in the person of a normal representative, so to speak, of the social group to which the speaker belongs. *Discourse is oriented toward the person addressed*, oriented toward what that person *is* (12:101).

The listener is thus either a present individual or the ideal image of an imaginary audience (G. H. Mead had coined the term "generalized other" to designate this last variant).

The sociability of the speaker is just as important, even though it is less manifest. After having taken the precautions discussed earlier (acts of sound production and acoustic perception are indeed individual, but they do not bear upon what is essential in language: meaning; there is also a biological and individual "I-experience" but unlike the "we-experience" it remains inaccessible), Voloshinov/Bakhtin asserts that there is nothing individual in what the individual expresses.

There is no experience outside its embodiment in signs. From the outset, then, there cannot even be question of a radical qualitative difference between interior and exterior. . . . It is not experience that organizes expression, but, to the contrary, expression that organizes experience, that, for the first time, gives it form and determines its direction (12:101). Outside material expression, no experience. More, expression precedes experience, it is its cradle (6:229).

A footnote to the last sentence assures that "this assertion is actually a follow-up to Engels's words" in *Ludwig Feuerbach*; perhaps a more distant source, shared by Engels and Voloshinov/Bakhtin could be seen here: Humboldt (otherwise the inspirer of "individualistic subjectivism"), for whom experience is preformed by the possibilities of expression. Whatever the source, as soon as the formative traces of expression are found within the expressible itself, there can no longer be any claim of an area devoid of some form of sociality (since words and other linguistic forms do not belong to the individual).

Only the inarticulate cry of the animal is really organized within the physiological apparatus of an individual entity. . . . But the most primitive human utterance, realized by an individual organism, is already organized outside of the latter, in the inorganic conditions of the social milieu, and that is so from the point of view of its content, its meaning, and its signification (12:101). Even the baby's crying is "oriented" toward the mother (12:104).

Another way of formulating this observation would be to say that every utterance can be considered as part of a dialogue; it will be noted that the word does not have here yet the meaning it will take in Bakhtin's later writings (dialogue between discourses), but rather its common meaning.

Verbal interaction is the fundamental reality of language. Dialogue, in the narrow sense of the term, is but one form, albeit the most important to be sure, of verbal interaction. But dialogue can be understood in a broader sense, meaning by it not only direct and *viva voce* verbal communication between two persons, but also all verbal communication, whatever its form (12:113). It could be said that all verbal communication, all verbal interaction takes place in the form of an *exchange of utterances*, that is, in the form of a *dialogue* (18:68):

This sociality of the utterance obviously fits in well with the explicitly Marxist intentions of Voloshinov/Bakhtin during this period; for him, as earlier for Medvedev/Bakhtin, it would be just as nefarious to forget the mediations that relate the social to the linguistic as to ignore the very existence of this relation. In one of the last articles signed Voloshinov, we can find this general outline:

1. *The economic organization of society*
2. *Social communication*
3. *Verbal interaction*
4. *Utterances*
5. *The grammatical forms of language* (18:66).

With these assumptions in place let us return to the description of the utterance. The first important consequence of the new framework is the necessity to distinguish radically between signification in language and signification in discourse, or to put it in the terminology Voloshinov/Bakhtin used at the time, between signification and *theme*. In itself, the distinction is not new, but what is new is the importance granted to the theme. For, indeed, the oppositions in currency then between usual and occasional signification, or between fundamental and marginal signification, or yet again between denotation and connotation, all err in that they privilege the first term, whereas in point of fact there is nothing marginal about discursive signification, or theme.

The term "signification" will be reserved here to the realm of language; the dictionary hoards the signification of words, whose first property is to be always identical to itself (since it is purely virtual); in other words, signification is, like other elements of language, reiterative.

By *signification,* in distinction to *theme,* we mean all the moments of the utterance that are *reiterative* and *identical unto themselves* in all their repetitions (12:120). In fact, signification signifies nothing, but only has the potentiality, the possibility of signifying in a concrete theme (12:122).

In opposition to this, the theme—just like the utterance of which it is part—is defined as unique, since it results from the encounter of signification with a context of enunciation equally unique.

Let us call the meaning of the utterance as a whole its *theme*. . . . In fact, the theme of the utterance is individual and nonreiterative, as is the case with the utterance itself. It is the expression of the concrete historical situation that engendered the utterance. . . . It follows that the theme of the utterance is determined not only by the linguistic forms that are its components (words, morphological and syntactical forms, sounds, intonation), but also by the extraverbal aspects of the situation. Were we to ignore these aspects of the situation, we would not be able to understand the utterance, as if we had ignored the most important words (12:119-20).

An essential feature of the theme, and therefore of the utterance, is that it is endowed with *values* (in the broad sense of the term). Conversely, signification and therefore language are alien to the axiological world.

Only the utterance can be beautiful, just as only the utterance can be sincere or false, courageous or timid, etc. All of these determinations bear only upon the organization of utterances and works, in conjunction with the functions they assume in the unity of social life, and especially in the concrete unity of the ideological horizon (10:117).

This evaluative dimension of the utterance is, in Voloshinov/ Bakhtin's eyes, more important than the semantic and the spatiotemporal dimensions. In a literary study, he asserts:

It is the *axiological* horizon that assumes the most important function in the organization of the literary work, and especially in that of its formal aspects (16:226).

Since it is part of the horizon shared by the interlocutors, the value judgment need not be made explicit (if it were, it would be because it had become questionable). Nonetheless, there is a certain number of means by which this judgment is expressed. First, there are non-verbal means.

Let us call all evaluation embodied in the material an *expression of values*. The human body itself will furnish the originary raw materials for this expression of values: *gesture* (the signifying movement of the body) and *voice* (outside of articulated language) (16:227-28).

Within language itself, one can distinguish semantic means from nonsemantic ones, such as the phonic, the foremost of which is *intonation*.

Intonation is always at the boundary between the verbal and the nonverbal, the said and the unsaid. In intonation, discourse enters in immediate contact with life. And it is in intonation first of all that the speaker enters in contact with his listeners: intonation is eminently social (7:253). Intonation is the most supple and most sensitive conduit of the social relations that exist between inter-locutors in a given situation. . . . Intonation is the *sound expression of social evaluation* (18:78).

Actually, intonation, like all the other aspects of the utterance, takes on a dual role:

All intonation is oriented in *two directions*: toward the listener, in his or her capacity as ally or witness, and toward the object of the utterance, as if it were a third participant assumed to be alive; the intonation abuses it or flatters it, belittles it or elevates it (7:255).

The semantic means for expressing evaluation are themselves sub-divided into two groups according to a dichotomy more familiar now than at the time, but the origin of which can be found in Kruszewski (and earlier, in classical rhetoric): selection versus combination.

We must distinguish two forms of the expression of values [in poetic creation]: 1. *phonic* and 2. structural [*tektonicheskuju*], whose functions are divided into two groups: first, *elective* (selective) and second, *compositional* (dispositional). The elective functions of social evaluation appear in the selection of lexical material (lexicology), in the choice of epithets, metaphors, and other tropes (the entire realm of poetic semantics), and, finally, in the selection of the theme, in the narrow sense of the term (the selection of the "content"). In this manner, almost all of stylistics and a part of thematics belong to the elective group.

The compositional functions of evaluation determine the hierarchical place of each verbal element in the whole of the work, its level, as well as the structure of the whole. All of the problems of poetic syntax, of composition, strictly speaking, and, finally, of *genre*, arise here (16:232).

Even the simplest utterance takes on, in Voloshinov/Bakhtin's eyes, the appearance of a little drama, whose minimal roles are: the speaker, the object, the listener. The verbal element is only the web from which the drama is played, or, as he puts it, the scenario.

Discourse is in some way the "scenario" of a certain event. The living understanding of the integral meaning of the discourse must *reproduce* this event of mutual relations between speakers; it must "play" it again, and the one doing the understanding takes on the role of listener. But to play this part, he or she must also understand clearly the position of the other participants (7:257).

Three aspects of this interaction seem to have the greatest importance in literary production.

(1) the hierarchical value of the character or of the event that forms the content of the utterance; (2) their degree of proximity to the author; (3) the interrelation of the receiver with the author on one side, and with the character on the other (7:266).

The first category deals with a "vertical" relation: is the character superior, inferior, or equal to the author? (This problematic, as is well known, is already present in Aristotle's *Poetics*.) The second lies on a "horizontal" dimension, and determines the selection of narrative forms: objective narration, confession, apostrophe. The third has to do with the interlocutor's position, which never coincides exactly with that of the author: the two may form an alliance, but sometimes the author sides with the character against the reader, at others it is the reader who associates himself with the character against the author, etc. It is important to bear in mind throughout this discussion that it is not a question of actual authors or readers but their roles such as they can be deduced from the utterance.

We will consider the author, the character, and the receiver, not outside the artistic event, but only insofar as they enter into the very perception of the literary work, insofar as they are its necessary constituents. . . . In return, all of the definitions that the historian of literature and society will propose in order to define the author and his characters (the biography of the author; more exact qualification of the characters, from chronological and sociological perspective, etc.) are obviously excluded here: they do not enter into the structure of the work, they remain outside of it. Similarly we will consider only such a receiver as the author himself considers, the one with respect to whom the work is oriented, and who, for this very reason, determines its structure, and not at all the real public that turned out to have actually read the work of this or that writer (7:260-61).

It is in the first book bearing Bakhtin's own signature—a study of Dostoevsky's work, that a final dimension of the utterance, one destined to play an even greater role, will appear: every utterance is also related to previous utterances, thus creating *intertextual* (or dialogical) relations. In the first edition of the book Bakhtin does not elaborate a general theory but rather a typology of utterances; it suffices for him to assert:

No member of a verbal community can ever find words in the language that are neutral, exempt from the aspirations and evaluations of the other, uninhabited by the other's voice. On the contrary, he receives the word by the other's voice and it remains filled with that voice. He intervenes in his own context from another context, already penetrated by the other's intentions. His own intention finds a word already lived in (13:131; in the second edition, of 1963, the two occurrences of "intention" will disappear to be replaced, respectively, by *osmyslenie*, interpretation, and *mysl'*, thought, cf. 32:270-71).

There is a paraphrase of this statement, and some others, in an article signed Voloshinov, with a variant that, at first glance, we could take for a typographical error were we not aware of the exceptional place accorded to *intonation* (which takes the place of "intention" here) in this thought.

For the poet, language is actually totally saturated with living intonations; it is completely contaminated by rudimentary social evaluations and orientations, and it is precisely with them that the creative process must struggle; it is precisely among them that one must select such or such a linguistic form, or this or that expression. The artist receives no word in linguistically virginal form. The word is already impregnated by the practical situations and the poetic contexts in which he has encountered it. . . . That is why the work of the poet, just as that of any artist, can only effect a few transvaluations, a few displacements in intonations, that the poet and his audience perceive against a background of previous evaluations and previous intonations (16:231).

Second Synthesis

Let us now consider the second synthesis, to be found in notes from the fifties published after Bakhtin's death under the following titles: "The Problem of the Genres of Discourse" and "The Problem of the Text," and in "Methodological Remarks" to the second edition of the Dostoevsky book, which provide a general summary. The frame of reference is no longer sociology, as it was thirty years earlier, but translinguistics, the new discipline Bakhtin wants to create and whose object is meant to be the utterance. Translinguistic entities differ qualitatively from linguistic ones. It would be a gross error to conceive of the utterance as of the same nature as the other units of linguistics, but of superior dimension, as the equivalent, let us say, of the paragraph.

The utterance, as a verbal entity, cannot be admitted as an entity of the last level or of the highest layer of the same linguistic structure (above syntax), because it enters into a universe of entirely different relations (dialogical) that are incompatible with the linguistic relations of the other levels. (On a certain plane, only the confrontation of the entire utterance with the *word* is possible.) The entire utterance is an entity, but no longer of language (or of "verbal flow" or of the "verbal chain"), but of *verbal communication* (30:304-5).

In this sense, the end-point of linguistics is but the point of departure of translinguistics; what was the end becomes a means here.

From the point of view of the extralinguistic aims of the utterance, all of linguistics is just a means (30:287).
    The object of linguistics consists only of the *matter*, of the means of verbal communication, and not of verbal communication itself nor of any of the following: the utterances as such; the (dialogical) relations that exist among them; the forms of verbal communication; and the forms of verbal genres (30:297).

Every utterance has two aspects: that which comes from language and is reiterative, on one hand, and that which comes from the context of enunciation, which is unique, on the other.

Two poles of the text. Every text presupposes a system of signs understandable to everybody (that is, conventional, valid within the limits of a given collectivity), a "language" (be it even the language of art). . . . To this system belong all the elements of the text that are repeated and reproduced, reiterative and reproducible, all that can be given outside of the text (the given). At the same time, however, every text (by virtue of constituting an utterance) represents something individual, unique, nonreiterative, and therein lies all its meaning (its intention, the reason why it has been created). It is the part of the utterance that has to do with truth, accuracy, the good, the beautiful, history. In relation to this aspect, all that is reiterative and reproducible turns out to be raw materials and means. To that extent, this second aspect, or pole goes beyond the boundaries of linguistics and philology. It is inherent to the text, but becomes manifest only in concrete situations and within sequences of texts (within verbal communication in a given realm). This pole is not tied to the (reiterative) elements of the system of language (that is, to signs), but to other (nonreiterative) texts by particular relations of a dialogical nature (and of a dialectical one, if the author is bracketed away) (30:283-84).

Schleiermacher had already distinguished between a *grammatical* perspective on texts (their confrontation with the system of the language, the identification of their reiterative part) and a *technical* one (the relation between the text at hand with the other texts of the same author, and other relevant data from his biography, etc.). Bakhtin will use yet other terms in his attempt to delineate this opposition.

The *given (dannoe)* and the *created (sozdannoe)* in the verbal utterance. The utterance is never the simple reflection or the expression of something that pre-exists it, is given and ready. It always creates something that had not been before, that is absolutely new and is nonreiterative, and that, moreover, always has a relation to values (truth, the good, the beautiful, etc.). But this thing comes into being only from a given thing (language; the observed real fact; the felt emotion; the speaking subject him/herself; what was already in his or her conception of the world, etc.) (30:299).

It is obvious that, in such a case, a purely linguistic approach of the utterance cannot suffice; it would ignore its most important features.

To study the *given* in the created (for example: the language, the already constituted general elements of the conception of the world, the reflected real facts, etc.) is far easier than the study of the *created* itself. Frequently, scholarly analysis as a whole winds up doing nothing more than making explicit all that is given, already present and constituted before the work (what was found, and not created, by the artist) (30:299).

Bakhtin will go so far as to distinguish two attitudes toward words, according to whether they are perceived as (already existing) units of language, or as units of discourse (new utterances). To name them, he uses terms that he may be borrowing from Benveniste,[1] but that he immediately integrates with themes that have always been dear to him:

The understanding—recognition of the reiterative elements of speech (that is, of language) and the interpretative understanding of nonreiterative utterance. . . . The word as means (language) and the word as interpretation. The interpreting word belongs to the realm of ends. The word as ultimate (supreme) end. . . . Laughter and the realm of ends (whereas the means are always serious). . . . Laughter and freedom. Laughter and equality (30:338, 339).

A later text returns to and elaborates further this distinction, this time in the context of a reflection on the epistemology of the human sciences:

Understanding. Articulation of understanding into separate acts. In real and concrete understanding, these acts are indissolubly intermingled in a unique process; but each separate act has ideational semantic unity (of content) and can be detached from the concrete empirical act. (1) The psychophysiological perception of the physical sign (the word, color, spatial form). (2) Its *recognition* (as either known or unknown). The understanding of its reiterative (general) *signification* in language. (3) The understanding of its *signification* in the given context (immediate as well as more remote). (4) Active and dialogical understanding (debate, agreement). Inclusion in a dialogical context. The moment of evaluation in understanding and the degree of its depth and its universality (40:361).

What comprises then the context of the enunciation? From the outset, three factors are indicated that permit the differentiation of an utterance from a sentence: in distinction to the latter, the utterance has a relation to a speaker, and to an object, and it enters into a dialogue with previously produced utterances.

To simplify things somewhat: purely linguistic relations (that is, the object of linguistics) are the relations of a sign to another sign or to other signs (that is, all systematic or linear relations between signs). The relations between utterances and reality, the actually speaking subject and other real utterances, relations that alone make utterances true or false, beautiful, etc., can never become the object of linguistics (30:302-3).

Here again, Bakhtin recalls the particular status of the speaker in question. She or he is referred to as the constitutive element of the enunciation, and therefore of the utterance; we also speak of the image of the author that can be deduced from the utterance, and, as a result, we have a tendency to project the second onto the first. Yet the distinction must be preserved. The author produces the entire utterance, and that includes "the image of the author"; but he, himself, is a producer and not a product, *natura naturans*, not *natura naturata*.

Even if the author-creator had created the most authentic autobiography or confession, he would nonetheless have remained, insofar as he had produced it, outside of the universe that is represented in it. If I tell (orally or in writing) an event that I have just lived, insofar as I *am telling* (orally or in writing) this event, I find myself already outside of the time-space where the event occurred. To identify oneself absolutely with oneself, to identify one's "I" with the "I" that I tell as impossible as to lift oneself up by one's hair. However realistic or truthful it may be, the represented universe can never be chronotopically identical with the real universe where the representation occurs, and where the author-creator of this representation is to be found. That is why the term "image of the author" seems to me unfortunate: all that in the work has become image, and that, therefore, enters into its chronotopes, is product, not producer. The "image of the author," if the author-creator is meant by it, is a *contradictio in adjecto*; every image is something produced and not something producing (39:405).

Let us return to the general description of the utterance. We have seen that the language, the speaker, the object, and other utterances all must be taken into account. Now enters the listener.

Discourse (as all signs generally) is interindividual. All that is said, expressed, is outside of the "soul" of the speaker and does not belong to him only. But discourse cannot be attributed to the speaker alone. The author (the speaker) may have inalienable rights upon the discourse, but so does the listener, as do those whose voices resonate in the words found by the author (since there are no words that do not belong to someone). Discourse is a three-role drama (it is not a duet but a trio). It is played outside of the author, and it is inadmissible to inject it within the author (30:300-301).

It is the relation between speaker and listener that determines what is commonly called the *tone* of an utterance (let us bear in mind the role previously played by intonation).

The exceptional role of tone. . . . The least studied aspect of verbal life. . . . The tone is not defined by the objective content of the utterance, nor by the experiences of the speaker, but by the relation of the speaker to the person of his partner (his rank, importance, etc.) (38:359).

In another series of notes, dating from 1952-1953, Bakhtin lists up to five constitutive features of the utterance, that are as many differences between utterance and proposition.

1) The boundaries of each concrete utterance, as a unit of verbal communication, are determined by changes in the subjects of the discourse, that is, the speakers (29:249).

2) Every utterance has a specific interior completion.

3) An utterance does not merely refer to its object, as a proposition does, but it *expresses* its subject in addition; the units of languages, in themselves, are not expressive. In oral discourse, a specific, *expressive* intonation marks this dimension of the utterance.

4) The utterance enters in relation with past utterances that had the same object, and with those of the future, which it foresees as answers.

5) Finally, the utterance is always addressed to someone.

These last three features are already known to us, since we have encountered them in Bakhtin's other expositions; let us consider then the formal criterion of the delineation of utterances (the alternation of speakers), as well as the idea of internal completion (which had come up in the discussion of genres in the book signed by Medvedev).

The completion [*zaveršennost*] of the utterance is, in a way, the interior aspect of the change in the subject of the discourse: the change can occur only because the speaker has said (or written) *all* that he wanted to say at this precise moment or in these circumstances. . . . The first criterion, and the most important, of the completion of the utterance, is the *possibility of responding to it*, more exactly and more broadly, of occupying with respect to it the position of responding. . . . The utterance must, in one way or another, be completed in order that we may react to it (29:255).

This completion is itself determined by three factors, and, correlatively, manifests itself on three planes: the plane of the object of which it is spoken (it is treated "exhaustively"); that of the discursive intention of the speaker, which we deduce from its very utterance but which allows us, at the same time, to measure its completion (that is Benveniste's "intended"); finally, that of the generic forms of the utterance (to which we shall return).

Signification, a property of language, is opposed here to *meaning*, a more familiar term that replaces the word "theme."

In all these cases, we are dealing not with the isolated words as a unit of language, nor with the *signification* of this word, but with the completed utterance and its concrete *meaning*, the content of this utterance (29:265).

It is meaning that relates the utterance to the world of values, unknown to language.

Isolated signs, linguistic systems, or even the text (as a semiotic entity) can never be true or false, or beautiful, etc. (30:303). Only the utterance can be accurate (or inaccurate), beautiful, just, etc. (30:301).

And, besides, meaning is nothing but the answer:

I call meaning the *answers* to the questions. That which does not answer any question is devoid of meaning for us. . . . The answering character of meaning. Meaning always answers some questions (38:350).

Model of Communication

One could summarize the preceding observations by reconstituting the model of communication as Bakhtin sees it, and by comparing it with a model more familiar to today's reader: that presented by Roman Jakobson in his essay "Linguistics and Poetics."

	Bakhtin			*Jakobson*	
	object			context	
speaker	utterance	listener	sender	message	receiver
	intertext			contact	
	language			code	

At first sight, two orders of differences are apparent. Jakobson gives independent status to contact, whereas it does not appear in Bakhtin's model, which, in turn, introduces the relations to other utterances (which I have labeled here "intertext"), something that is missing in Jakobson. Then, there is a set of differences that could be considered purely terminological. The terms used by Jakobson are more general (semiotic and not just linguistic) and they betray his contacts with information engineers. "Context" and "object" both correspond to what other theoreticians of language call the "referent." On a closer look, however, it will be noticed that the differences are more important, and that the terminological discrepancy betrays a fundamental opposition. Jakobson presents his notions as describing "the constitutive factors of any verbal event, of any act of verbal communication."[2] But for Bakhtin, there are two radically distinct "events"; to such an extent that they demand two autonomous disciplines: linguistics and translinguistics. In linguistics, one begins with words and grammatical rules, and one ends with sentences. In translinguistics, one starts with sentences and the context of enunciation and one obtains utterances. Thus, to formulate propositions concerning "any verbal event," an event of language as well as of discourse, would be, in Bakhtin's perspective, a useless enterprise. The schema I have drawn up here must be handled carefully: the "language" factor must not be put on the same plane as the others; similarly, it cannot account for the fundamental difference between discourse and language, namely, the existence of a common horizon between speaker and listener.

There is more. It is not by chance that Bakhtin says "utterance" rather than "message," "language" rather than "code," etc.: he is deliberately rejecting the language of engineers in speaking of verbal communication. Such a language carries the risk of making us see linguistic exchange in the image of something like the work of telegraph operators: one person has a content to transmit, and encodes it with the help of a key and transmits it through the air; if contact is established, the other decodes it with the same key, thus recovering the initial content. Such an image does not correspond to discursive reality: the latter institutes the speaker and listener with respect to each other; properly speaking, they do not even exist in such capacity before the utterance. That is why language is something other than a code, and that is why it would be inconceivable for Bakhtin to isolate "contact" as a factor among others; the entire utterance is contact but in a much stronger sense than is to be found in radiotelegraphy or even electricity. Discourse does not maintain a uniform relation with its object; it does not "reflect" it, but it organizes it, transforms or resolves situations.

Curiously enough, there is in the Medvedev book a page that criticizes the Jakobsonian model of language some thirty years before that model was formulated; nevertheless, it was written in response to the theories of the Formalists, a group to which Jakobson belonged.

What is transmitted is inseparable from the forms, manners, and concrete conditions of the transmission. The Formalists presuppose tacitly, however, in their interpretation, an entirely predetermined and fixed communication, and an equally fixed transmission.

This could be expressed schematically as follows: there are two members of society, A (the author) and B (the reader); the social relations between them are, for the time being, unchangeable and fixed; we also have a ready-made message X, which must simply be handed over by A to B. In this ready-made message X, there is distinguished the "what" ("content") and the "how" ("form"), literary discourse being characterized by the "objective of expression" ("how") [this is a quotation from Jakobson's first published text]. The proposed schema is radically wrong.

In reality, the relations between A and B are in a state of permanent formation and transformation; they continue to alter in the very process of communication. Nor is there a ready-made message X. It takes form in the process of communication between A and B. Nor is it transmitted from the first to the second, but constructed between them, like an ideological bridge; it is constructed in the process of their interaction (10:203-4).

We find in 1928 a precise prefiguration of the critiques addressed today to the purely "communicational" model of language. Bakhtin does not fail, in any case, to reformulate this critique himself, forty years later, and to extend it to all of nascent semiotics:

Semiotics prefers to deal with the transmission of a ready-made message by means of a ready-made code, whereas, in living speech, messages are, strictly speaking, created for the first time in the process of transmission, and ultimately there is no code (38:352).

Heterology

If we go now from the model of the particular utterance to the set of utterances that constitute the verbal life of a community, one fact appears, to Bakhtin, more striking than all others: the existence of *types of utterances*, or discourses, in a relatively high but nonetheless limited number. Two excesses are to be avoided here: to recognize only the diversity of languages and ignore that of utterances; to imagine that this last variety is individual and therefore unlimited. The stress is not on the plurality but on the difference (there is no need to conceive of a higher level unit of which all the discourses would be variants; Bakhtin takes a stand against the idea of a unification). To name this irreducible diversity of discursive types, Bakhtin introduces a neologism, *raznorečie*, which I translate (literally, but with the aid of a Greek root) by *heterology*, a term that inserts itself between two other parallel coinages, *raznojazyčie*, heteroglossia or diversity of languages, and *raznogolosie*, heterophony or diversity of (individual) voices.

Every utterance, it will be recalled, is oriented toward a social horizon, composed of semantic and evaluative elements; the number of these verbal and ideological horizons is high but not unlimited; and every utterance necessarily falls within one or more types of discourses determined by a horizon.

In language, there is no word or form left that would be neutral or would belong to no one: all of language turns out to be scattered, permeated with intentions, accented. For the consciousness that lives in it, language is not an abstract system of normative forms but a concrete heterological opinion on the world. Every word gives off the scent of a profession, a genre, a current, a party, a particular work, a particular man, a generation, an era, a day, and an hour. Every word smells of the context and contexts in which it has lived its intense social life; all words and all forms are inhabited by intentions. In the word, contextual harmonies (of the genre, of the current, the individual) are unavoidable (21:106).

The preceding lists indicate that the stratification of language into discourses does not occur along a single dimension. In the most detailed examination of heterology he has conducted ("Discourse in the Novel," a text dating from 1934-1935), Bakhtin distinguishes up to five types of differentiation: by genre, profession, social stratum, age, and region (dialects, in the strict sense of the term). Let us note that social classes do not play a role different from that of professions and age classes: it is a factor of diversification among others. We shall return later to the theory of genres, developed with respect to literature, that corresponds to the least obvious differentiation, since it is purely verbal. Let us indicate here though that the ignorance of genre is specifically raised as a shortcoming of linguistics in general and of Saussure in particular:

Saussure ignores the fact that outside the forms of language there exist also *forms of combination* of these forms; in other words, he ignores discursive genres (29:260).

And let us bear in mind that Voloshinov/Bakhtin never confines himself to literary genres only; he even sketches out, but without developing, a general typology of discourses, of which literary discourse would be but one instance.

In observing social life, we can easily isolate, outside of the artistic communication already discussed, the following types: (1) the communication *of production* (in the factory, in the shop, in the kolkhoz, etc.); (2) the communication *of business* (in offices, in social organizations, etc.); (3) familiar [*bytovoe*] communication (encounters and conversations in the street, the cafeteria, at home, etc.); and finally (4) *ideological* communication in the precise sense of the term: propaganda, school, science, philosophy, in all their varieties (18:66-67).

Heterology is, in a way, natural to society; it arises spontaneously from social diversity. But just as the latter is constrained by the rules imposed by the single State, the diversity of discourses is fought against by the aspiration, correlative to all power, to institute a common language (or rather a speech).

The category of common language is the theoretical expression of historical processes of linguistic unification and centralization, the expression of the centripetal forces of the language. The common language is never given but in fact always ordained, and at every moment of the life of the language it is opposed to genuine heterology. But at the same time, it is perfectly real as a force that overcomes this heterology; imposes certain limits upon it; guarantees a maximum of mutual comprehension; and becomes crystallized in the real, though relative, unity of spoken (daily) and literary language, of "correct language" (21:83-84).

As can be seen, Bakhtin will speak also, with respect to the tendency toward unification, of "centripetal force," and, with respect to heterology, of "centrifugal force." The different discourses themselves further, for variable reasons, one or the other force. The novel (what Bakhtin calls by this word), for example, reinforces heterology in distinction to poetry; that is because heterology is solidary of the representation of language, a constitutive feature of the novel.

Whereas the principal species of poetic genres arise in the current of unifying and centralizing centripetal forces of verbal and ideological life, the novel and the genres of literary prose that are bound to it have historically taken form in the current of decentralizing, centrifugal forces (21:86).

Therefore the periods in which the novel flourishes are periods of weakening central power.

The embryos of novelistic prose appear in the heteroglottic and heterological world of the Hellenistic era, in imperial Rome, in the process of disintegration and decadence of the verbal and ideological centralism of the medieval Church. Similarly, in modern times the flourishing of the novel is always connected with the decomposition of stable verbal and ideological systems, and, on the other hand, to the reinforcement of linguistic heterology and to its impregnation by intentions, within the literary dialect as well as outside of it (21:182).

One may well be led to wonder here to what extent Bakhtin follows the rules of prudence he laid a few years earlier, and whether he does not skip a few intermediate links in the relation between social structures and linguistic forms. Besides, could it not be argued conversely that the flowering of the modern novel coincides, in the seventeenth and eighteenth centuries, with efforts to establish a common national language?

Traditional stylistics ignores this sort of assembly of languages and style into a higher unit; it does not know how to approach the particular social dialogue of languages in the novel. Stylistic analysis therefore does not consider the novel as a whole, but only one or another of its subordinate stylistic planes. The scholar bypasses the basic distinctive feature of the novel as a genre; he substitutes another object of inquiry, and instead of novelistic style, he actually analyzes something altogether different. He transposes an orchestrated symphonic theme to the piano (21:76-77).

Bakhtin lists several other examples of powerlessness before the heterological:

Aristotle's poetics, the poetics of Augustine, the medieval Church's poetics of "the common language of truth," the Cartesian poetics of Neo-Classicism, the abstract grammatical universalism of Leibniz (the idea of a universal grammar), Humboldt's ideologism of the concrete—all of these, whatever their differences of shading, give expression to the same centripetal forces of sociolinguistic and ideological life, and serve the same project of centralizing and unifying the European languages (21:84).

The surprise in this series of names is Humboldt, a distant inspirer of Bakhtin, as we have seen, and, in addition, a defender of linguistic diversity (*Verschiedenheit*). The explanation must be as follows. For Humboldt there are only two types of diversity: the diversity of languages and the diversity of individuals (language gives expression to the national spirit, and the utterance, to individual spirit). He forgets the decisive element: social diversity. Beyond classical unicity and Romantic infinity, Bakhtin looks for a middle way: the way of typology.

Chapter Five
Intertextuality

Definition

There is no utterance without relation to other utterances, and that is essential. The general theory of the utterance is, in Bakhtin's eyes, but an unavoidable detour to get him to the study of this facet of the question. The term he uses to designate the relation of every utterance to other utterances is *dialogism*, but this key term is, as one could expect, loaded with such an embarrassing multiplicity of meanings that I have preferred to proceed somewhat as I did earlier in transposing "metalinguistics" into "translinguistics": I will therefore use, for the more inclusive meaning, the term "intertextuality" introduced by Julia Kristeva in her presentation of Bakhtin, setting aside the denomination *dialogical* for certain specific instances of intertextuality, such as an exchange of responses by two speakers, or Bakhtin's conception of human personality. Bakhtin himself invites such a terminological distinction in the following remark:

These relations [between the discourse of the other and the discourse of the I] are analogous to (but certainly not identical with) the relations between the exchanges of a dialogue (29:273).

At the most elementary level, any and all relations between two utterances are intertextual.

Two verbal works, two utterances, in juxtaposition, enter into a particular kind of semantic relation, which we call dialogical (30:297). Dialogical relations are (semantic) relations between all the utterances within verbal communication (30:296).

Intertextuality belongs to discourse and not language, and therefore falls within the sphere of competence of translinguistics and not that of linguistics. However, not all relations between utterances are necessarily intertextual. Logical relations must be excluded from dialogism (for example: negation, deduction, etc.); in themselves, they do not imply intertextuality (though the latter may be bound to them); the same is obviously true of purely formal, or linguistic, relations in the strict sense (anaphora, parallelism, etc.).

These [dialogical] relations are profoundly specific and cannot be reduced to relations of a logical, linguistic, psychological, or mechanical type, or to any other kind of natural relations. It is a particular type of *semantic* relations, whose parts must be constituted by *whole utterances* (or utterances considered whole, or potentially whole), behind which stand (and in which express themselves) actual or potential speaking subjects, the authors of the utterances in question (30:303).

The end of the last sentence is important: in the intertextual relation, the utterance is considered as evidence of the subject.

In order to become dialogical, logical relations and objectal semantic relations must achieve material existence, as was said earlier, that is, they must enter into another sphere of being: become *discourse*, that is utterance, and receive an *author*, that is the creator of the utterance, whose position is in turn expressed by the utterance. In this sense, every utterance has an author, whom we hear in the very utterance as its creator. . . . The dialogical reaction endows with personhood the utterance to which it reacts (32:246).

This does not mean, it will be recalled, that the utterance gives expression to the inimitable individuality of its author. The utterance at hand is perceived rather as the manifestation of a conception of the world, while the absent one as that of another conception; the dialogue takes place between the two. For example:

In the process of literary creation, the mutual illumination of a native language and a foreign language [if it occurs in the work] underscores and objectifies the "conception of the world" facet of both languages, as well as their internal form, and their respective systems of values. For the consciousness creating the literary work it is obviously not the phonetic system of the native language, or its morphological particularities, or even its abstract vocabulary, that appear in the field illuminated by the foreign tongue, but precisely that which makes of the language a concrete and absolutely untranslatable conception of the world: specifically, the style of the language as a totality (24:427).

Every representation of language puts us in contact with its utterer; to make us "conscious" of what language is, is to have us identify who speaks within it. This "personhood" covers the gamut from an entire linguistic community (the use of English connotes the subject of "Englishness") to the subject of individual forms of expression, and passing through the subject of dialects and styles in all their variety. The individual forms are reserved for the private use of language; literary representation, on the other hand, cannot rely upon any intimacy on our part with the characters that it puts forward, and therefore deals only in collective subjects of enunciation.

All these [nonliterary] forms, even where they come closest to literary representation, as, for example, in some two-voiced rhetorical genres (parodic stylizations), are oriented upon the individual's utterance. . . . In the authentic novel, one can feel behind every utterance the nature of social languages with their internal logic and necessity. . . . The image of such a language in the novel is the image of the social horizon, of the social ideologeme, welded to its discourse, to its language (21:167-69).

No utterance is devoid of the intertextual dimension. Already in one of his earliest publications, Voloshinov/Bakhtin remarked that every discourse refers to at least two subjects, and thus to a potential dialogue.

"Style is the man"; but we can say: style is, at least, two men, or more precisely, man and his social grouping, incarnated by its accredited representative, the listener, who participates actively in the internal and external speech of the first (7:265).

In the later writings, Bakhtin will particularly insist on another patent fact: whatever the object of speech, this object, in one way or another, has always already been said, and it is impossible to avoid encountering the discourse previously held upon this object.

The dialogical orientation is obviously a characteristic phenomenon of all discourse. It is the natural aim of all living discourse. Discourse comes upon the discourse of the other on all the roads that lead to its object, and it cannot but enter into intense and lively interaction with it. Only the mythical and totally alone Adam, approaching a virgin and still unspoken world with the very first discourse, could really avoid altogether this mutual reorientation with respect to the discourse of the other, that occurs on the way to the object (21:92).

Not only have words always already been used and carry within themselves the traces of preceding usage, but "things" themselves have been touched, at least in one of their previous states, by other discourses that one cannot fail to encounter. The only distinction that can be drawn in this regard is not between discourses endowed with intertextuality and those devoid of it, but between two roles, one weak and one strong, that intertextuality can be called on to play. Bakhtin proceeds then to make an inventory of all the types of discourse in which the intertextual dimension is essential: daily conversation; law; religion; the human sciences (it will be recalled that their distinctive features lie in their having to do with texts, with which they enter into dialogue; rhetorical genres, such as political discourse; and so on. However, the role of intertextuality is minimal in the natural sciences: the discourse of the other, to the extent it occurs, is generally confined between quotation marks (21:150-67).

Absence of Intertextuality?

Bakhtin knows perfectly well that the intertextual dimension is omnipresent, yet, at times, he is tempted to inscribe it into a simple opposition where the "intertextual" utterance would face a nonintertextual one. An examination of these attempts and their (relative) failure is instructive.

1) Dialogic and Monologic

Naturally, the first term to come to mind in opposition to "dialogue" is "monologue." But we have seen that Bakhtin uses "dialogic" and "dialogism" in a very broad sense that makes even the monologue dialogical (i.e., it has an intertextual dimension). In this respect, Bakhtin's hesitation in characterizing Tolstoy's writing is significant. In 1929, he asserts it is monologic, and the assertion is further amplified in the second edition of the book on Dostoevsky (1963).

Tolstoy's universe is monolithically monological. . . . In his universe, there is no second voice alongside that of the author; hence, no problem of the combining of voices, or of a special status for the author's viewpoint (13, 67-68; cf. 32:75).

But in the meantime, in 1934-1935, and again in 1975 when these other lines appear, Bakhtin upholds the contrary:

In Tolstoy, discourse is characterized by a clear internal dialogism, in the object as much as in the reader's horizon, a dialogism whose semantic and expressive particularities are acutely perceived by Tolstoy (21:96).

In fact, the opposition of the dialogic and the monologic gives way to an internal cleavage of the dialogic, which assumes different forms (this allows the maintenance of a special place for Dostoevsky, privileged instance of dialogism).

After Dostoevsky, polyphony makes a powerful entrance into all of world literature. . . . In dialogism, especially in reference to the subjectivity of his characters, Dostoevsky crosses a kind of threshold, and his dialogism attains a (higher) new quality (30:291).

2) Prose and Poetry

From as early as the first edition of the *Dostoevsky*, and especially with "Discourse in the Novel," prose, which is intertextual, is opposed to poetry, which isn't. Poetic complexity, Bakhtin would say, locates itself between the discourse and the world; that of prose, between the same discourse and its utterers.

In the poetic image in the narrow sense (image-trope) all action—the dynamics of the image—takes place between the word (in all of its aspects) and the object (in all of its complexity). The word bathes in the inexhaustible riches and the contradictory variety of the object, in its "virginal" and as yet "unnamed" nature; it does not presuppose anything outside the frame of its context (to which are added, of course, the treasures of the language). The word forgets the history of the object's contradictory emergence into awareness, as it forgets the heterological present condition of this awareness. For the prose-artist, on the contrary, the object makes manifest, above all, the social and heterological variety of its names, definitions, and evaluations (21:91).

It isn't that the representation of discourse, and therefore of its utterer, is impossible in poetry, but it just isn't aesthetically valorized there as it is in prose.

Most poetic genres (in the strict sense of the term) do not avail themselves of the internal dialogism of discourse artistically; it does not enter into the "aesthetic object" of the work; it is conventionally stifled in poetic discourse. In the novel, on the other hand, it becomes one of the most essential features of prosaic style, and receives a specific artistic elaboration (21:97).

Should poetry attempt to avail itself of this resource, it is immediately drawn to the side of the novel. Bakhtin constantly cites Pushkin's *Eugene Onegin* as an example of the novel, not of poetry. Or again, when poetry represents discourse, it does it in clear-cut forms, in somewhat scientific fashion (it is the direct style of the character, comparable to a quotation, whereas prose favors more subtle forms such as "double-voiced" or "hybrid" discourse whose description we will study later. In conclusion, Bakhtin will say that, in poetry "discourse upon doubt must be without doubts" (21:99): there may be complexity in the object but the discourse must remain crystal clear.

The reasons of this opposition may be seen in the fact that the poem *is* an uttering act whereas the novel *represents* one.

The language of the poet is *his own* language; he is wholly immersed in it, and inseparable from it; he makes use of each word, form, and expression according to its intended purpose ("without quotation marks" as it were) that is, as the pure and unmediated expression of his own intention (21:98). Every word must express in unmediated and direct fashion the poet's design; there must be no distance between the poet and his discourse (21:109). [The prose writer, for his part,] does not speak in a given language, from which he distances himself to a greater or lesser degree, but he speaks *through* language, as it were, a language that has gained in thickness, become objectivized, and moved away from his mouth (21:112).

The poet fully takes upon himself his speech act, which becomes an enunciation in the first degree, not represented, without quotation marks. The prose writer represents language, introduces a distance between himself and his discourse; his act of uttering is double (one could see in this opposition a foreshadowing of the ideas that Käte Hamburger would develop twenty years later in *Logik der Dichtung*).

3) The Novel and other genres

The novel is, for Bakhtin, the crowning achievement of prose; therefore it is in the novel that intertextuality appears most intensely.

The phenomenon of internal dialogism, as we have said, is present to a greater or lesser extent in all the realms of the life of discourse. But if, in nonliterary prose (everyday, rhetorical, scholarly), dialogism ordinarily stands apart as a particular kind of act and becomes established in plain dialogue or in other forms, clearly marked at the level of composition and designed to set off the discourse of the other for polemical purposes — then in *literary* prose, and especially in the novel, dialogism energizes from within the very mode in which the discourse conceives of its object and its means of expressing it, transforming the semantics and the syntactical structure of the discourse. Here the dialogical reciprocal orientation becomes, so to speak, an event of discourse itself, animating it and dramatizing it from within in all of its aspects (21:97).

More: intense intertextuality is the most salient feature of the novel.

The fundamental object, specific to the novel as genre, and the one that gives it its stylistic originality, is *man speaking* and his *discourse* (21:145). It is not the image of man himself that is characteristic of the genre of the novel, but the image of language. (21:149)

Dostoevsky's work is the jewel of this crown, the purest embodiment of this basic tendency of the novel.

Unlike most artists, Dostoevsky does not restrict his attention to the representational and expressive functions of discourse—the art of recreating, like an artifact, the social and individual specificity of the discourse of characters. What matters to him most of all is the dialogical interaction of the discourses, whatever their linguistic particularities. The main object of the representation he constructs is discourse itself, and especially *meaningful* discourse. Dostoevsky's works are a discourse upon discourse, addressed to discourse (32:538; cf. 13:188).

What is the novel opposed to? The answer is: to all the genres that, for this purpose, are considered to be "direct."

Every novel is, to a varying extent, a dialogical system of representations of "languages"; styles; concrete consciousnesses inseparable from language. In the novel, language does not merely represent: it is itself an object of representation. Novelistic discourse is always self-critical, and therein lies the difference between the novel and all the "direct" genres—the epic, the lyric, and drama in the strict sense (24:416).

We shall return to the problems raised by Bakhtin's theory of genre; let us note here, though, that, in other texts, Bakhtin sketches an opposition between the novel and myth, two "genres" that seem to him to constitute the opposite poles of the intertextual continuum. Myth implies a transparency of language, a coincidence of words and things; the novel starts out with plurality of languages, discourses, and voices, and the inevitable awareness of language as such; in this sense, the novel is a basically self-reflexive genre.

The absolute fusion of discourse and concrete ideological meaning is, without a doubt, one of the basic constitutive features of myth, determining, on the one hand, the development of mythological representations, and on the other determining the specific apprehension of linguistic forms, significations, and stylistic combinations. . . . Verbal and ideological decentering occurs only when a national culture sheds its closure and its self-sufficiency, when it becomes conscious of itself as only *one* among other cultures and languages. This new awareness will then sap the roots of the mythological sense of language, based on the notion of an absolute fusion of ideological meaning with language (21:180-81).

4) Literature and nonliterature

This opposition is, generally speaking, alien to Bakhtin's way of thinking; we have seen him chastise the Formalists for having granted undue autonomy to "poetic language." It is significant in this respect that although one of the early texts bears the title, "Discourse in Life and Discourse in Poetry," it does not make much of this opposition: the only difference to receive attention concerns the necessity of a more explicit form of communication in literature (owing to the absence of the immediate context). And Bakhtin asserts then: "The bases and the potentialities of the artistic form to come are already present in ordinary *everyday discourse*" (7:249). Or again: "The key to the understanding of the linguistic structure of literary utterances is to be found in the simplest utterances" (18:75).

It is only at the very beginning of his career that Bakhtin makes explicit reference to the dichotomy literature/nonliterature; and he does so in terms at once familiar and opaque: literature is language in its totality, the summoning forth of all of the potentialities of language.

Poetry needs all of language, all of its aspects, and all of its elements; it does not neglect a single nuance of the linguistic word. No area of culture, with the sole exception of poetry, needs language in its totality. . . . Only in poetry does language reveal all of its potential, for the demands made upon it here are at their highest (4:46).

Or again, literature is that which, within language itself, allows language to be overcome.

Artistic creation, defined with respect to its basic material, consists in the overcoming of this material (4:46). The artist frees himself from language in its linguistic determination not through negation but by *means of its immanent perfecting. . . . Immanent overcoming defines formally the relation to the basic material, not only in poetry but in all of the arts* (4:49).

And in a text from the same epoch:

The artist works the language but not as language; in that capacity, he overcomes it. . . . (The word must no longer be felt as a word.) . . . The basic intention of the artist can be described as an effort to *overcome the basic material* (3:167).

Bakhtin will eventually abandon this distinction of Romantic origin. But in a late text, he sets up an equivalency, certainly not meant to be exclusive, between literature and intertextuality as representation of language.

To what extent is a discourse purely single-voiced and without any objectal character, possible in literature? Can a discourse in which the author does not hear the other's voice, in which there is no one but the author and all of the author, can such a discourse become the raw material of a literary work? Isn't a certain degree of objectal character a necessary condition for any style? Doesn't the author always find himself *outside* of language in its capacity as the material of the literary work? Isn't every writer (even the purest lyric poet) always a "playwright" insofar as he distributes all the discourses among alien voices, including that of the "image of the author" (as well as the author's other *personae*)? It may be that every single-voiced and nonobjectal discourse is naive and inappropriate to authentic creation. The authentically creative voice can only be a *second* voice in the discourse. Only the second voice—*pure relation*, can remain nonobjectal to the end and cast no substantial and phenomenal shadow. The writer is a person who knows how to work language while remaining outside of it; he has the gift of indirect speech (30:288-89).

Authentic voice can only be a second voice. . . . Obviously these lines are a sequel to an internal dialogue in Bakhtin himself: the distribution between prose and poetry set up earlier is annulled here. Even the purest of lyric poetry no longer avoids the representation of its own language. Intertextuality is never absent; only some of its forms can be.

Typologies

Now I shall sum up briefly the various typologies Bakhtin works out from his analysis of the representation of discourse within discourse.

Matters are relatively simple at the time of *Marxism and the Philosophy of Language*. Voloshinov/Bakhtin gives his attention to only one form of representation—*reported discourse*—and he concentrates on the description of the relation between the quoting discourse and the quoted discourse. To do so, he has recourse to an opposition formulated by Wölfflin for his typology of styles in painting: they are the "basic concepts" of *linear* and *pictural*. Here are Wölfflin's definitions:

Although in the phenomenon of linear style, line signifies only part of the matter, and the outline cannot be detached from the form it encloses, we can still use the popular definition and say for once as a beginning—linear style sees in lines, painterly in masses. Linear vision, therefore, means that the sense and beauty of things is first sought in the outline—interior forms have their outline too—that the eye is led along the boundaries and induced to feel along the edges, while seeing in masses takes place where the attention withdraws from the edges, where the outline has become more or less indifferent to the eye as the path of vision, and the primary element of the impression is things seen as patches. In the one case, the line means a track moving evenly round the form, to which the spectator can confidently entrust himself; in the other, the picture is dominated by lights and shadows, not exactly indeterminate, yet without stress on the boundaries.[1]

In Wölfflin, these categories will come into opposition with "classical" and "baroque," an indication of the Romantic origin of this dichotomy. The Romantics are indeed notorious for having distinguished between the great periods of history on the basis of their capacity to reconcile opposites or draw them apart; such is certainly the basis of the opposition between "Classical" and "Romantic."

It is easy to imagine the result of the projection of this opposition on the relation between quoting discourse and quoted discourse.

What direction of development can the dynamic of interrelations between the discourse of the author and the discourse of the other take? There are two main ones. First, the basic tendency of an active reaction to the discourse of the other may lead the subject to seek to preserve his own integrity and his own authenticity. In such a case, language can tend to enclose the discourse of the other in clear and stable boundaries. Commonplaces and their variants are used: to isolate the discourse of the other in the strictest and clearest fashion; to exclude the intonations of the author; to abridge and develop his individual linguistic particularities. . . . If we use the term introduced by Wölfflin in art history, we could call this first direction taken by the dynamic of the verbal interrelation between the discourse of the author and the discourse of the other, a *linear style (der lineare Stil)* of transmission of the discourse of the other. Its basic tendency consists in the creation of clear and external contours for the discourse of the other, which is itself at the same time poorly individualized internally (12:117-18).

At the other pole, we have the "pictural" style:

The context of the author attempts to break up the compactness and closure of the other's discourse, to absorb it, to erase its borders. This style of transmission of the discourse of the other can be called *pictural*. Its tendency consists in erasing the clear-cut character of the contours of this discourse. In this instance, the discourse itself is individualized to a far higher degree; the perception of the different aspects of the other's utterance becomes finer and more nuanced. Not only the objective meaning of the utterance, or the assertion it contains, are perceived, but also all the linguistic peculiarities of its verbal embodiment receive attention (12:199).

Within such a style, one of the voices can be dominant, a possibility that leads to further subdivisions.

In a study from the same period, Voloshinov/Bakhtin examines the forms of *interior dialogue*. The principle of diversification is different here: it is a question of the role played by the second voice when we talk to ourselves. In most instances, this second voice is that of a typical representative of the social group to which we belong, and the conflict between the two is that lived by the individual confronting his or her own norm. A second instance puts together two voices with equal status; such a situation implies that one feels that one belongs to two social groups at the same time, and that the conflict between them has not yet been decided by history. If finally, in a third instance, the second voice does not occupy a stable position but consists in an incoherent series of reactions exclusively determined by the circumstances of the moment, then the human being in question has lost his frame of reference, his appurtenance to a definite group, and is in danger of losing his mind.

In especially unfavorable social conditions, such a cleavage between the person and the ideological environment that provides its nourishment can ultimately lead to the complete disintegration of consciousness, to disorder or insanity (18:71).

It is in the first edition of his *Dostoevsky* that Bakhtin puts forward a general classification of the different ways of representing discourse—a classification that will be barely revised in the second edition of the book. Simplifying it somewhat, one could sum it up in the following diagram (I give in paranthesis the most common example for each species).

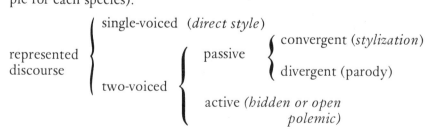

In the discussion of single-voiced discourse, Bakhtin encounters anew some problems evoked by Voloshinov/Bakhtin, but he does not reuse the typology previously sketched out.

The represented discourse of a character may vary in degree of objectality. It suffices to compare, for example, how Prince Andrey talks in Tolstoy with the talking done by Gogol's characters, such as Akaky Akievich. As the immediate orientation of the characters' discourse toward the object grows stronger, and, conversely, its objectal character weakens, the relations between the discourse of the narrator and the discourse of the character begin to resemble those between the replies of a dialogue (13:109-10 and 32:251-52; instead of "orientation" the earlier edition always has "intention").

Two-voiced discourse is characterized by the fact that not only is it represented but it also refers simultaneously to two contexts of enunciation: that of the present enunciation and that of a previous one. Here the author

can also use the discourse of the other toward his own ends, in such a way that he imprints on this discourse, that already has, and keeps, its own orientation, a new semantic orientation. Such a discourse must, in principle, be perceived as being another's. A single discourse winds up having two semantic orientations, two voices (13:111 and 32:253).

The difference between the *active* and *passive* species has to do with the role assumed by the earlier (or generally, the other) utterance.

In stylization as in parody . . . the author uses the discourse of the other to give expression to his own orientations. In the third species [the active], the discourse of the other remains on the outside of the discourse of the author, but the latter takes it into account and establishes a relation with it. Here the discourse of the other is not reproduced with a new interpretation, but it acts, has influence, and, in one way or another, determines the discourse of the author, all the while remaining outside of it (13:121 and 32:261; here "interpretation" takes the place of "intention").

Each category thus defined is further subdivided and illustrated with examples drawn from Dostoevsky's works.

The articulation of the different problems that the representation of discourse brings to the fore constitutes the main theme of "Discourse in the Novel," written some five years after the *Dostoevsky*. The great difference with respect to the previous classification is that Bakhtin no longer seeks to unify in a single schema all the forms of representation, but rather considers three aspects of the phenomenon, entirely independent from each other.

First, there can be a variation in the *locus* where the discourse of the other can be "encountered": it may be the object of which we speak or the addressee we direct our remarks to (this resembles somewhat the opposition of the "active" and "passive" forms in the earlier diagram). We recall still that, for Bakhtin, there is no object unsullied by prior denomination.

Instead of the virginal fullness of an inexhaustible object, the prose writer is faced with a multiplicity of routes, roads and paths that have been laid down in the object by social consciousness. Along with the internal contradictions of the object itself, the prose writer comes to discover as well the social heteroglossia that *surrounds* the object, the Tower of Babel confusion of languages that goes on around any object. The dialectics of the object are interwoven with the social dialogue surrounding it. For the prose writer, the object is a condensation of heterological voices among which his own voice must also resound; these voices create the background necessary for his own voice, without which his literary nuances would not be perceived, and without which they "do not sound" (21:91-92).

The confrontation with the discourse of the other is of a "paradigmatic" nature here, in Saussure's sense: it is a conflict between several substitutable denominations of the same object.

But there is another possible encounter, this time with the potential discourse of the interlocutor, within a new syntagmatic context; the discourse of the other belongs to the future here rather than the past.

The speaker seeks to orient his discourse, and even the horizon that has determined his discourse, in relation to the horizon of the other, the one who does the understanding, and he enters into dialogical relations with some aspects of this second horizon. . . . Very often, especially in rhetorical forms, the aiming toward the listener and the related internal dialogism of the discourse simply occult the object: persuading an actual listener redirects available attention and interferes with the discourse's creative work on the object (21:95-96).

Second, the discourse of the other can be summoned forth, especially in a novel, in several different *forms*. Bakhtin lists the following: discourse not assumed by the actual narrator ("unreliable" in the terminology of Wayne Booth); representation of the narrator, in a situation of oral and written type; direct style and "characters' zones"; finally, embedded genres. The first category is subdivided into such forms as parody, stylization, or irony (which is presented here as a variant of a discourse with a dual enunciation). The notion of "character zone" makes its first appearance in this context.

Heteroglossia is also diffused in the authorial discourse that surrounds the characters, creating very specific *character zones*. These zones are formed from the characters' semi-discourses, from various forms of hidden transmission for the discourse of the other, by the words and expressions scattered in this discourse, and from the irruption of alien expressive elements into authorial discourse (ellipsis, questions, exclamation). Such a zone is the range of action of the character's voice, intermingling in one way or another with the author's voice (21:129-30).

Third, one can finally vary the *degree* of presence of the other's discourse. Bakhtin puts forward a differentiation of three degrees. The first is full presence, or explicit dialogue. At the other end—the third degree—the other's discourse receives no material corroboration and yet is summoned forth: it is because it is held available in the collective memory of a given social group; such is the case of parody, stylization, and another form of summoning forth that Bakhtin calls "variation."

Here one language only is actualized in the utterance, but it is presented in the *light of another language*. This second language is unrealized, and it remains outside of the utterance (21:174).

Between these two, there is a second degree, doubtlessly of greatest interest for Bakhtin, who calls it "hybridization": it is a generalization of free indirect style.

We call hybrid construction any utterance that belongs, by its grammatical (syntactic) and compositional features, to a single speaker, but that actually contains intermingled within it two utterances, two manners of speaking, two styles, two "languages," two semantic and axiological horizons (21:118).

These two voices, Bakhtin reminds us, can only be social, not individual.

Bakhtin returns to these questions one last time in "The Problem of the Text." No systematic classification is to be found here, but rather the evocation of several aspects of dialogism, all capable of variation. Thus, the *degree* of explicitness that can go from open dialogism to the most discrete allusion; of the *evaluation*, whether positive or negative, that we make of someone else's discourse.

The narrow interpretation of dialogism as debate, polemic, parody. Those are the most obvious forms but also the most rough-hewn. Trust in someone else's discourse; pious acceptance (authoritarian discourse); disciples; the search for and the (forced) extraction of a deeply lying meaning; *agreement*; its infinite gradations and nuances (but not the logical limitations and the purely objectal reservations); the superimposition of one meaning upon another, of one voice on another; reinforcement by fusion (without identification); the combining of multiple voices (soundtrack); complementary understanding; exceeding the limits of understanding; etc. (30:300).

We can also distinguish between forms that are *intentional* and those that aren't in intertextual dialogue.

Two utterances, whatever they may be, as soon as they are set side by side on the semantic plane (not as objects or as linguistic examples) will find themselves in a dialogical relation. But it is a particular form of unintentional dialogism (for example, a selection or various utterances upon the same issue by different scholars or sages, from different periods as well) (30:246).

Finally, the *distance* between authorial voice and someone else's voice can vary as well.

The word used in quotation marks, that is felt and used as alien, and the same word (or another) without quotation marks. The infinite gradation in the degrees of strangeness (or appropriateness) between words, their different degree of distance in relation to the speaker. Words are set on different planes, at different distances, in relation to the plane of the author's words. Not only free indirect discourse, the various forms of alien discourse: hidden, semi-hidden, scattered, etc. (30:300).

The most detailed and the most systematic presentation of the entirety of these problems is indeed to be found in "Discourse in the Novel": it is the end-point of Bakhtin's reflection in the field of "translinguistics."

Chapter Six
History of Literature

Categories

An initial hypothesis concerning the history of literature is formulated by Voloshinov/Bakhtin in *Marxism and the Philosophy of Language*; it is a pure projection of the typology of styles that he had just drawn up (which follows Wölfflin and his opposition of the linear versus pictural). The variants of these two great stylistic types correspond to well-delinated historical periods.

> Summing up all we have said about the possible tendencies in the dynamic re-lation between authorial discourse and the discourse of the other, we can distin-guish the following periods: *authoritarian dogmatism*, characterized by a linear and impersonal monumental style in the transmission of the discourse of the other (the middle ages); *rationalist dogmatism*, with an even clearer linear style (seventeenth and eighteenth centuries); *realistic and critical individualism*, with its pictural style, and a tendency to inject, into the other's discourse, the replies and commentaries of the author (late eighteenth century and nineteenth cen-tury); and finally, *relativistic individualism*, with the disintegration of the au-thor's own context (contemporary period) (12:121).

These four great periods of literary history betoken, in effect, a moderate and an extreme form of each of the two styles, the linear and the pictural.

The context of this opposition will remain relatively stable through-out Bakhtin's work; but its role will begin to alter as early as in the next text devoted to a study of the same issue, namely "Discourse in the Novel." It could be said that a hypothesis concerning history places itself, depending on its ambitions, in one of three stages or degrees: either, in the case of a weak hypothesis (degree zero), one limits oneself to a *history of events*, that is to the simple recording of facts, without worrying about their articulation; or—next degree—one develops an *analytic history*, where one makes use of a limited number of categories to describe historical facts; or finally, in the case of the strongest hypothesis, one practices *systematic history*, and one is no longer content to analyze events by means of the same categories, but one asserts the existence of an order in change, which, ultimately, could lead to foreseeing the future: the Hegelian model is the best known example of such a hypothesis.

The formulation advanced by Voloshinov/Bakhtin put him in the ranks of the proponents of the systematic approach: not only were all styles defined by the opposition linear-pictural, but there was also a direction to the evolution: we go precisely from medieval linearity to modern picturality. It will be noted, though, that for Voloshinov/ Bakhtin there is no third, synthetic term as we find in Hegel, and this fact is revealing; for him, oppositions will always have an unsurmountable character.

Still, in "Discourse in the Novel," Bakhtin moves from the strong, systematic hypothesis to a weaker, analytic one. There are still two stylistic poles, but both have been present since Antiquity: the "linear" is exemplified by the Hellenistic novel (Bakhtin's favorite example is *Leucippe and Clitophon* of Achilles Tatius); the "pictural" by a series of lesser genres that lead, in Antiquity, to two famous works, the *Satyricon* of Petronius and *The Golden Ass* of Apuleius. Each of these two styles undergoes multiple transformations, instances of which can be found equally in all periods. For example, the medieval romance, the Baroque novel, the sentimental novel of the eighteenth century, all belong to the first pole; the fabliau, the picaresque novel, the comic novel, though their contemporaries, all belong to the second pole. The only exception to this nonsystematic schema, and it is far from insignificant, is to be found in the present period, which, according to Bakhtin, is dominated entirely by what he called the pictural.

The tenor of the opposition may have remained that of the conceptual duality introduced by Wölfflin, but it has become, at the same time, more precise and more specifically literary. Bakhtin believes that, in every epoch and in all circumstances, there occurs a dialogue of styles, based on heterology. But this dialogue can take

HISTORY OF LITERATURE □ 77

place *in absentia*, that is between the homogeneous style of the work and the other dominant styles of the period (external heterology); or *in praesentia*, within the work, which thus contains the heterology within itself; the first dialogue obviously corresponds to linear style and the second, to the pictural.

The primary characteristic [of the first tradition] is that it is monolingual and stylistically monolithic (in a more or less consistent fashion); heterology remains *outside* the novel; nonetheless it determines it, acting as a dialogical background to which the language and the world of the novel react polemically and apologetically. . . . The second lineage, to which belong the greatest representatives of the novel as a genre (its greatest subgenres as well as the greatest individual works) injects social heteroglossia into the body of the novel and leaves to it the orchestration of its meaning, frequently giving up altogether any pure and unmediated authorial discourse (21:186).

This opposition could also be described in the dynamic of its becoming:

Novels of the first stylistic lineage approach heterology from above, it is as if they *descend* unto it (the sentimental novel stands apart here, somewhere between heterology and the higher genres). Novels of the second lineage, on the contrary, approach heterology from below: they rise from the depths of heterology to overtake the higher spheres of literary language. In both instances, the point of view of heterology prevails upon that of literariness (21:211).

I shall make an exception here to my rule of avoiding comparisons between Bakhtin and later writers because a comparison seems so much called for. In *Mimesis*, written some ten years after "Discourse in the Novel" (but published thirty years earlier), Erich Auerbach also reviews the history of European literature in the light of the opposition of two stylistic attitudes: the separation of styles (*Stiltrennung*) and the mixture of styles (*Stilmischung*); both are equally present since Antiquity, their prototypes being the *Iliad* for the first and the Bible for the second (Auerbach does not confine himself to the novel); at every moment of history one can find representative examples of each of the two attitudes, but modern times are marked by a victory of the mixture of styles. Naturally, Auerbach could not be ignorant of Wölfflin's opposition, where the second term goes beyond the Baroque to characterize the modern period). The closeness between Bakthin and Auerbach is also apparent in their common, and continuing, interest in the problem of the literary representation of the real. The author of *Mimesis* would not have disavowed the titles that Bakhtin was giving to his manuscripts: "The *Bildungsroman* and its Signification in the History of Realism"; "Francois Rabelais in the History of Realism."

In subsequent works, Bakhtin will again alter his formulations while retaining the opposition. The same penchant for hypothetical reconstructions of a past inaccessible to observation—a penchant that led him, a few years earlier, to embrace the theories of Marr upon the origin of language, leads him, at the time of his work on the chronotope, to an image of primitive man and the distinctive features of his mental life. This primitive world is characterized by working and living collectively; by the importance of the role granted to natural rhythms (the growth of plants, the change of the seasons); the orientation toward the future; the domination of the concrete; continuous and cyclical time; the equal value of the elements of life. With the rise of class society, this model of life will be abandoned and repressed; but it will reemerge in the form of a popular culture opposed to official culture (cf. 23:356-66).

We may well question both the mythical image reconstructed by Bakhtin, and its identification, in the historical period, with a *popular* culture (wasn't culture, in the strict sense, especially in those times, the preserve of an elite fundamentally alien to the "people"?); but we must take note of the shift away from a stylistic opposition between the linear and the pictural, or between a dialogism *in absentia* or one *in praesentia*, to an anthropological and cultural opposition between official and popular culture, or, as Bakhtin puts it in his *Rabelais*, where the most complete description of this popular culture is to be found, between serious culture and the culture of laughter (*smekhovaja*).

[In the Renaissance and the Middle Ages] an immense world of forms and manifestations of laughter opposed the official and serious tone of medieval ecclesiastical and feudal culture (25:6).

In the chapter added to the second edition of the Dostoevsky, devoted to the problem of genre, we can find Bakhtin's last formulations on this issue:

It can be said, with some restrictions to be sure, that medieval man in a way led *two lives*: one *official*, monolithically serious and somber; beholden to strict hierarchical order; filled with fear, dogmatism, devotion, and piety; the other, of *carnival* and the *public place*, free; full of ambivalent laughter, sacrileges, profanations of all things sacred, disparagement and unseemly behavior, familiar contact with everybody and everything (32:173).

This popular and comic culture is apparent in several forms: (1)

rites and spectacles, such as carnival; (2) comic verbal works; (3) the familiar discourse of the public place. Of these forms, Bakhtin has a special appreciation for carnival, because it concentrates and reveals all the features of comic popular culture. "*Carnival*, with its whole complex system of images, was the purest and fullest expression of comic popular culture" (25:90). Hence, the frequent use of the term "carnivalesque," applied by synecdoche to the whole of this culture. A synonymous expression, to be found in the *Rabelais*, is "grotesque realism"; the strong term here is "grotesque," which is opposed to "classical" (making the latter a member of the series: "official," "serious," etc.).

The *Rabelais* provides a list of characteristic features of popular and comic culture: a material and corporeal principle of life; disparagement and debasement, hence parody; ambivalence: confusion of death with rebirth; the necessary relation to time and becoming. In the book on Dostoevsky, nearly the same table can be found; its elements are: free and familiar contact between persons; the attraction of the eccentric, the surprising, the bizarre; misalliances, the reunion of opposites; profanation and debasement (see 32:164-65). The essence of carnival lies in change, in death-rebirth, in destructive-creative time; carnivalesque images are basically ambivalent.

These characteristics are most directly observable in a certain period: the Middle Ages (and, in part, the Renaissance). They can be extrapolated, however (we are still in analytic history), and their avatars identified in any period: the carnivalesque is foreshadowed by the comicoserious genres of Antiquity (the most important of which are the Socratic dialogues and Menippean satire, and its highest expression is to be found in the modern period in the polyphonic novel of Dostoevsky.

In his evocation of two stylistic lines, turned into two forms of culture, Bakhtin does not act like an impartial historian; his sympathies for the mixture of styles and for "popular" culture are obvious. He justifies himself in part by recalling that the popular and heterogeneous tradition has been largely ignored—for reasons easily comprehensible: history and scholarship partake of the same "official," "serious," and "classical" ideology; as a result they insist on those things that approximate their ideal. In this view, Bakhtin's work would remedy a lacuna, hence his concentration on the description of "popular" culture.

But this explanation of a quantitative predominance does not justify the value judgments that always favor the same cultural pole, and neither does the frequent implication that the "people" constitute a supreme value. Were we to accept it, it would be easy to assert that leaving the "safety valve" of the carnivalesque open is the best means for the dominant class to perpetuate its tyranny. The explanation of Bakhtin's obvious preference is, I think, somewhat different, and calls into play his epistemological, psychological, and aesthetic beliefs: human existence itself is a "mixture of styles, an irreducible hetero-geneity." The representation will work only if there is an analogy be-tween the represented object and the representing medium; art and literature, forms of representation, will work better the truer they are, that is the more they resemble their object, hetergeneous human existence. That is the reason why, ultimately, the "pictural" tradi-tion is preferable to the "linear" one.

Genres

"Poetics must begin with genre" (10:175).

This precept occurs as early as the Medvedev/Bakhtin book of 1928; genres are a constant preoccupation of Bakhtinian thought and come to figure for it as the key concept of literary history. It will be recalled that one of Bakhtin's projects of the fifties and sixties was entitled *The Genres of Discourse* (only a brief sketch remains). The attraction of Bakhtin in his youth for this notion is easily explain-able: it fits in well with his two initial methodological choices; the nonseparation of form and content, and the predominance of the so-cial over the individual. Because genre is, first of all, on the side of the collective and the social. And Bakhtin will explain his interest in the "stylistics of genre" in the following terms:

The separation of style and language from genre is largely responsible for the fact that only individual overtones of style, or those of literary currents, are the privileged objects of study, while the basic social tone is ignored. The great his-torical destinies of literary discourse, tied to the destiny of genres, are over-shadowed by the petty vicissitudes of stylistic modification, themselves tied to individual artists and particular currents. For this reason, stylistics has been de-prived of an authentic philosophical and sociological approach (21:72-73).

Stylistics must become a stylistics of genres, and thus integrate it-self into sociology. "The true poetics of genre can only be a sociolo-gy of genre" (10:183).

Genre is a sociohistorical as well as a formal entity. Transforma-tions in genre must be considered in relation to social changes.

All these particularities of the novel . . . are conditioned by a moment of breach in the history of European humanity: the breach by which it emerges from a socially closed and semipatriarchal state, to enter new circumstances that promote international and interlinguistic links and relations (27:455).

Second, the notion of genre is more fertile, and therefore more important, than those of school or current; precisely because, one could imagine, it always has a formal reality as well.

The historians of literature do not see, beyond the surface agitation and splashes of color, the great and essential destinies of literature and language, whose chief, foremost characters are the genres, while currents and schools are lesser characters (27:451).

The privileged position of the notion of genre is linked to this mediating function.

The utterance and its types, that is, the discursive genres, are the transmission belts between social history and linguistic history (29:243).

At the same time, it could be asserted, with some regret, that Bakhtin seems unaware of the problem posed by the use of the same term ("genre") for a linguistic and translinguistic reality on one hand, and a historical one on the other; he uses the word equally in both contexts, thus giving rise to some problems, as we shall see in the case of the novel.

The unseverable bond between a genre and its linguistic reality makes it always possible to relate literary genres to other discursive genres. For the notion of genre is not the exclusive prerogative of literature; it is rooted in the everyday use of language.

The question, the exclamation, the command, the request, those are the most typical everyday complete utterances. . . . In salon chatter, light and without consequences, where everyone is at home, and where the main differentiation (and separations) among those present (those whom we call the "audience") is between men and women—in this situation a particular form of generic completion occurs. . . . Another type of completion is worked out in the conversation between husband and wife, brother and sister. . . . Every stable daily situation comprises an audience organized in specific fashion, and therefore includes a definite repertory of small everyday genres (12:98-99).

This omnipresence of genres has nonetheless not prevented widespread ignorance of their existence (particularly with respect to intimate and familiar genres); Bakhtin himself in fact did not go beyond the formulation of this general program; we find in his writings the recommendation to study "the preliterary germs of literature (in language and in rite)" (38:345) as well as the idea that a distinction must be drawn between the "primary" genres of language and the "secondary" genres of literature (a distinction that parallels Andre Jolles's opposition of "simple forms" and "complex forms"):

It is particularly important to draw attention here to the absolutely essential distinction between primary (single) discursive genres and secondary (complex) ones. This is not a functional distinction. The secondary (complex) discursive genres—novels, drama, scientific research of all types, great journalistic genres, etc.—emerge in conditions of more complex and relatively developed, organized, cultural communication: essentially written communication, of an artistic, scientific, social, and political, etc. kind. In the process of their formation, they absorb and transform the various primary (simple) discursive genres that arose in conditions of unmediated verbal communication (29:239).

But what exactly is a genre? It is one of the fundamental notions of translinguistics, the discipline that studies the stable, nonindividual, forms of discourse.

Every particular utterance is assuredly individual, but each sphere of language use develops its own *relatively stable types* of utterances, and that is what we call *discursive genres* (29:237).

How to analyze the notion of genre? The first elements of an answer are to be found in the Medvedev/Bakhtin book. Genre originates in the dual orientation of every utterance, orientation toward its object and toward an interlocutor.

An artistic entity of any type, that is, of any genre, is related to reality according to a double modality; the specifics of this double orientation determine the type of this entity, that is its genre. The work is oriented, first, toward its listeners, and recipients, and toward certain conditions of performance and perception. Second, the work is oriented toward life, from the inside so to speak, by its thematic content. Every genre, in its own way, orients itself thematically toward life, toward its occurrences, its problems, etc. (10:177).

There follows a rapid examination of the forms taken by this orientation in both cases. But, although the two cases are set, in principle, on the same plane, Medvedev/Bakhtin's attention is already concentrated more upon the relation between work and world, and it is with respect to this relation that he introduces the notion, essential here, of *completion*. By definition, the world is unlimited, endowed with innumerable properties; genre makes a selection among them, sets a model of the world, and breaks up the infinite series.

For the theory of genres, the problem of completion is among the most vital

(10:175). The subdivision of particular arts into genres is determined in large measure by the types of completion of the entire work. Each genre is a particular manner of constructing and completing the whole, since it is essential, let us stress this, to achieve thematic completion, and not a conventional one at the level of composition only (10:176). Every genre that is an essential genre is a complex system of ways and means of apprehending reality in order to complete it while understanding it (10:181). A genre is the set of means for a collective orientation in reality, aiming for completion (10:183).

Genre, then, forms a modeling system that proposes a simulacrum of the world.

Every genre has its methods, its ways of seeing and understanding reality, and these methods are its exclusive characteristic (10:180). The artist must learn to see reality through the eyes of the genre (10:182).

When Bakhtin returns to the question of genre, ten years later, his conception has become more focused and restricted. There is no longer question, with respect to genres, of an orientation toward the interlocutor, but only of a relation between the text and the world — of the model of the world put forward by the text. This modeling is analyzed at the same time into its constitutive elements, which turn out to be two: space and time.

The field of representation changes from genre to genre and among the periods of literary evolution. It is organized differently and it delineates itself differently as space and time. This field is always specific (27:470).

To designate these two essential categories that always occur in conjunction with each other, Bakhtin coins the term of *chronotope*, that is, the set of distinctive features of time and space within each literary genre. Given the definition of genre, the two words, genre and chronotope, will become synonymous.

In literature, the chronotope has an essential *generic* signification. It can be stated categorically that genre and generic species are precisely determined by the chronotope (23:235).

It must immediately be added that Bakhtin does not use the notion of chronotrope in restricted fashion, and does not limit it simply to the organization of time and space, but extends it to the organization of the world (which can be legitimately named "chronotope" insofar as time and space are fundamental categories of every imaginable universe). All the same, in the very text in which Bakhtin works out this notion, there is a noticeable process of amplification, since he begins with pertinent remarks on the organization of space and time in the Greek novel, and ends with a description of Rabelais's "chronotope" in which the relation to the temporal and spatial dimension is not always obvious.

Rabelais' varied series can be reduced to the following basic groupings: (1) series of the human body in its anatomical and physiological dimensions; (2) human clothing series; (3) food series; (4) drink and drunkenness series; (5) sex series (copulation); (6) death series; (7) excrement series (23:319).

When, in his last texts, he evokes again the problem of genre, Bakhtin rapidly passes by the general definition ("genre is defined by the object, the goal, and the situation, of the utterance" [38:358]), and lingers on another point: the reality of genre in the life of a society. Bakhtin appears to have considered two aspects of the problem. On the one hand, generic rules have, within a society, a reality comparable to that of linguistic rules: both may be unconscious but they exist nonetheless.

We speak only through certain discursive genres, that is, all our utterances have some relatively stable and typical *forms* enabling them to achieve totality. . . . Linguistic forms and the typical forms of utterances, that is discursive genres, integrate our experience and our consciousness, according to strict relation of one with the other (29:257).

And just as linguistic rules can be violated, generic rules can be ignored, but not without some consequences.

Many people with a remarkable knowledge of the language feel totally powerless in some areas of communication, precisely because they do not know all the practical forms of the genres that have currency in those areas. Frequently a man who knows remarkably well the discourse of different cultural spheres, who knows how to give a lecture, lead scholarly debate, and who is to be commended for his interventions on public issues, is reduced to silence or intervenes in a most awkward fashion in a social conversation (29:259).

On the other hand, genre has a historical dimension: it is not only an intersection of social and formal properties but also a fragment of collective memory.

Genre lives in the present, but it always *remembers* the past, its beginnings. Genre is the representative of creative memory in the process of literary evolution, which is precisely why genre is capable of guaranteeing the *unity* and the *continuity* of this evolution (32:142). The same generic universe is manifest at the *beginnings* of its evolution in the Menippean satire, and at its *peak*, reached in

Dostoevsky. But we already know that the beginnings, that is, the generic archaisms, are maintained in renewed form in the higher levels of the evolution of the genre. Moreover, the more elevated the genre, the more complex it has become and the more, and the better, it remembers its past (32:161-62).

It is indeed a case of collective and not individual memory, and its content may even remain unknown to the individual; but this content is inscribed in the formal properties of the genre.

Does this mean that Dostoevsky took Menippean satire as his starting point *directly* and *consciously*? Certainly not. . . . Somewhat paradoxically, it can be said that it is not Dostoevsky's subjective memory, but the objective memory of the very genre he used, that preserved the particularities of Menippean satire (32:162). Cultural and literary traditions (including the most ancient ones) are preserved and continue to live, not in the subjective memory of the individual, nor in some collective "psyche," but in the objective forms of culture itself (including linguistic and discursive forms); in this sense, they are intersubjective and interindividual, and therefore social; that is their mode of intervention in literary works—the individual memory of creative individuals almost does not come into play (39:397).

The Case of the Novel

Going from these general considerations to the genre on which Bakhtin focused his attention throughout his life, namely the novel, one cannot help but feel a certain malaise. We have already come across the novel in the course of the presentation of various of Bakhtin's theses: it is the highest incarnation of intertextual play, and it gives heterology the greatest room for action. But heterology and intertextuality are nontemporal categories that can be applied to any period of history; how is their omnipresence to be reconciled with the necessarily historical nature of the genre? Our malaise is likely to increase when we notice that Bakhtin's favorite examples— those that keep recurring in his writings and allow him to identify the genre specifically—are not works to which the genre of the novel is ordinarily associated (such would be works of Fielding, Balzac, or Tolstoy, authors barely mentioned), but those of Xenophon and Menippus, Petronius and Apuleius. If the novel is reduced to intertextuality and heterology, these works are certainly representative; but then, speaking of the novel in Antiquity, one can do no more than note, in that period too, the presence of intertextual play and heterological plurality. What is gained by this new designation? It seems that the concept of the novel is so essential to Bakhtin that it escapes his own rationality, and that the use of the term is due to an attachment of a primarily affective nature, that does not bother about the reasons of its fixation. So that a question is forced upon us: is the novel, in the Bakhtinian sense of the term, really a genre? We have seen, besides, that a genre is to be defined by its chronotope; yet, in Bakhtin, there is never question of a *single* novelistic chronotope.

This presumption of a singular status for the notion of novel increases when one notes that all of the characteristics of the novel are taken by Bakhtin, without notable alteration, from the great Romantic aesthetic, the reflections of Goethe, Friedrich Schlegel, and Hegel, as if a failure to achieve genuine integration of the notion into his own system authorized such a massive and uncritical borrowing. Let us look a little closer at Bakhtin's description of the novel, and its relation to his Romantic predecessors.

For Bakhtin, the novel is a genre like no other, because each of its instances is ultimately irreducibly individual (a contradiction, indeed, of the very notion of genre).

The essential point is that, unlike other genres, the novel has no canon: only particular examples play a role in history, but not the canon of the genre as such (27:448).

This assertion is a direct reference to Friedrich Schlegel:[1]

Every novel is a genre in itself (KA, XVIII, 2, 65). Every novel is an individual entity for itself, and therein lies the essence of the novel (KA, III, p. 134).

Schlegel affirmed in addition, as does Bakhtin, that the novel results from the admixture of all the genres that existed before it.

The idea of a novel, as it is established by Boccaccio and Cervantes, is the idea of a romantic book, a romantic composition, where all the forms and all the genres are mixed and interwoven. In the novel, the principal mass is furnished by prose, more diverse than that of any genre set by the Ancients. There are historical parts, rhetorical parts, parts in dialogue; all these styles alternate, they are interwoven and related in the most ingenious and the most artificial way. Poems in all genres, lyrical, epic, didactic, as well as romances, are scattered throughout the whole and embellish it in a varied and exuberant profusion and diversity in the richest and most brilliant fashion. The novel is a poem of poems, a whole texture of poems. It is obvious that a poetic composition of this kind, produced from such varied elements and forms where external conditions are not strictly limited, allows a much more artificial poetic interweaving than the epic of drama, insofar as the first requires a unity of tone while the second must be easily summed up and apprehended, since it is to be offered to intuition (KA, XI, p. 159-160).

Or, more concisely: "The novel is a mixture of all poetic kinds, of natural poetry without artifice, and of the mixed genres of artistic poetry" (LN:55).

Socratic dialogues, Bakhtin will say, are the novels of Antiquity. Schlegel asserted similarly: "Novels are the Socratic dialogues of our day" (KA, II, *Lyceum* 26). According to Bakhtin, the novel is the youngest of the "great" genres (the category of "great" or "basic" genres will never be made explicit by him).

Among the great genres, only the novel is younger than writing and the book, and it is the only one organically adapted to the new forms of silent perception, that is reading. . . . The study of other genres is analogous to the study of dead languages; the study of the novel, to the study of modern languages, and young ones at that. . . . The novel is simply a genre among others. It is the only genre in a state of becoming among genres that have reached completion long ago and are already partly dead (27:448).

But the idea is already present in this manifesto of Romantic aesthetic that is the fragment 116 of the *Athenaeum*, whose author is again F. Schlegel.

Other poetic genres are now completed and can now be fully dissected. The poetic genre of the novel is still in becoming (KA, II, *Athanaeum* 116).

And it is known that for Schlegel ("Gespräch über die Poesie") "a novel is a romantic book."

Last born, the youngest of all, the novel is naturally the genre that does best today, and it dominates modern literature to the point that it is confused with modern literature. Bakhtin writes: "In some measure, it is with it and in it that is born the future of all literature" (27: 481). And Schlegel: "All modern poetry draws its original coloration from the novel" (KA, II, *Athenaeum* 146).

In spite of the assertion that the novel is not really a genre, Bakhtin attempts to make more precise the opposition between the novel and the other "great" genres; and, at this point, he inevitably comes across the problematic triad of the lyric, the epic, and the dramatic.

We have already seen the difficulties encountered by Bakhtin, in his own perspective, in redefining the opposition novel-poetry ("poetry" in this context being the functional equivalent of "lyric"). If we take into account the distinction between two stylistic lines in the history of Western literature (*in absentia* and *in praesentia* dialogism), this opposition becomes even more fragile: isn't all of lyric poetry related to the first stylistic line, the one that maintains the homogeneity of the text while entering into dialogue with external heterology?

Bakhtin devotes the most attention to the distinction between epic and novel, in a text by that very name. To tell the truth, already the introduction to this debate is worrisome; for, as soon as he announces his project, Bakhtin refuses to grant the epic any specificity.

The three constitutive features of the epic that we have just described are equally proper, to a greater or lesser extent, to other high genres of classical Antiquity and of the Middle Ages (27:461).

But let us examine the definitions of the novel and the epic that are put forward. First, the novel:

I try to reach the basic structural features of this genre, the most plastic of all—features that have determined the direction of its own changes as well as the direction of its influence and of its action on the rest of literature. I find three such basic characteristics that distinguish the novel radically from all other genres: (1) the stylistic three-dimensionality of the novel, tied to the polyglot consciousness that actualizes itself in it; (2) the radical transformation of the temporal coordinates of the literary image in the novel; (3) the new zone of construction of the literary image in the novel, namely, the zone of maximum contact with the present (contemporary reality) in its openendedness (27:454-55).

The first of these characteristics is already known to us: discourse here is not only representing but also represented, object of representation; it is the question of the novel's tendency to reproduce a plurality of languages, discourses, and voices. This characteristic made an appearance in the opposition between the novel and (lyric) poetry, and it will not be commented upon here, in the confrontation with the epic. It is the two other characteristics ("already thematic moments of the structure of the genre of the novel," 27:456) at work in the opposition of the novel and the epic, that receive further definition from Bakhtin:

(1) a national epic past—in Goethe's and Schiller's terminology the "perfectly past"—serves as the epic's object; (2) national legend (and not personal experience and the free invention that flows from it) serves as the source for the epic; (3) an absolute epic distance separates the epic world from contemporary reality, that is from the time in which the singer (and author and his audience) lives.

It will be noted that "epic," the term under definition, appears twice in the definition itself ("epic past," "epic distance"); in sum, the category is an anthropological one before it becomes literary.

These features—two for the novel against three for the epic—that allow the setting up of an opposition between the novel and the epic, are not clearly distinguished among themselves later on, and, in fact, can be reduced to a single great opposition: possible or impossible continuity between the time of the (represented) utterance and the time of (representing) uttering. The other characteristics of the two universes, epic and novelistic, derive from there.

The formally constitutive feature of the epic as a genre is rather the transferral of a represented world in the past and the appurtenance of this world to the past. . . . To portray an event on the same temporal and axiological plane as oneself and one's contemporaries (and, therefore, from personal experience and invention) is to accomplish a radical transformation, and to step out of the world of the epic into the world of the novel (27:456-57).

A whole slew of other characteristics of the novel (and of the epic) are brought in relation to this basic opposition. The representation of the author within the novel becomes possible; the novel requires a well-delineated beginning and end, whereas the epic can do without them; the novel valorizes the couple knowledge—lack of knowledge; the epic embodies unity, the novel diversity, etc. These remarks are of considerable interest, but we may well wonder whether they are all applicable to a genre, to a historically circumscribed entity, or rather whether they are not universally transgeneric and transhistorical categories. The reference to Goethe in one of the quoted passages may help us answer this question. In the text entitled "Über epische und dramatische Dichtung," written in 1797 and published in 1827, cosigned by Schiller and Goethe, but actually written by Goethe alone, the epic is indeed placed into an opposition, not to the novel, though, but to *drama*. "The epic poet relates the event as *perfectly past*, while the playwright represents it as *perfectly present*" (*Jubiläumsausgabe*, vol. 36, p. 149).

The opposition between epic and drama is clearly rooted here in the dichotomy of "relating" and "representing" (which in turn refers back to Plato's opposition of *diegesis* and *mimesis*. But those are two modalities of discourse: how can one ask of them that they take on the status of historical and generic characteristics? Looked at from another perspective, the same distinction underlies parallel developments in Hegel, who is also mentioned by Bakhtin in these pages.

For the content as well as the representation of what he [the epic poet] narrates is intended to appear as removed from himself as a subject and as a closed reality in itself. The poet is not permitted to enter into a completely subjective unity with this closed reality—either with respect to the objective self, or with respect to its presentation. The third mode of representation [the drama] finally binds the two earlier ones together in a new totality, in which we see before us an objective development as well as its origin from within individuals. Thus the *objective* represents itself as belonging to the *subject*; simultaneously, however, the subjective is represented on the one hand in its transition to a real expression, and on the other hand as the lot which passion brings about as the necessary result of its own action.

It is not only drama that thus shares the properties of the "novel" as defined by Bakhtin; so does the epic. I shall invoke but one example from Bakhtin himself. First, here is how, in the study on the chronotope, he characterizes the epic: "The internal aspect fuses with the external; man is wholly outside" (23:367).

Yet, in the same pages, Rabelais' work is presented as the purest incarnation of the novelistic; here is Bakhtin's description:

It must be stressed that in Rabelais there is absolutely no aspect of interior individual life. In Rabelais, man is wholly outside. A certain limit in the exteriorization of man is reached here. . . . Action and dialogue give expression to all that is within man (23:388).

In a text from the same period, the novelistic and the epic are no longer in a relation of opposition, but one appears to be a species of the other. "The great epic form (the great epic), including the novel . . . (22:224). The novel (and the great epic in general) . . ." (22:227).

Some twenty years later, Bakhtin seems to have reversed himself. Now it is the epic that is a single aspect of the novelistic:

In somewhat simplified and schematic fashion, it could be said that the novelistic genre has three basic roots: epic, rhetorical, *carnivalesque* (32:145).

On the other hand, we never find (unless it is in the unpublished materials) the confrontation we await, between the novel and drama.

The not very coherent, and ultimately irrational, character of Bakhtin's description of the genre of the novel is a strong indication that this category does not occupy its own place in the system. The intersection of two categories, present intertextuality and temporal continuity, does not provide a definition of a sufficiently specific object so that it may be located historically. Such a definition, which will inevitably be general, will not attain the complexity of the reality it is meant to apprehend; a genre appears at a certain period, and at no other. "Representing" or "relating" does not define a genre, but categories of discourse in general. The same applies to what Bakhtin had proposed as the constitutive features of the "novel."

What he described under this name is not a genre, but one or two properties of discourse, whose occurrence is not confined to a single historical moment.

Novelistic Subgenres

Bakhtin's generic analysis may be baffling with respect to the novel, but it proves apposite to the study of novelistic subgenres. They receive his attention during the thirties especially, in a series of investigations that could be divided into two groups: those bearing on the representation of discourse, and those devoted to the representation of the world. These two series are apparently independent of each other, and, in the end, we have *three* lists of the main novelistic subgenres.

In "Discourse in the Novel," the enumeration of the subgenres occurs in the context of the discussion on the two stylistic lines whose conflict characterizes the history of the European novel. We get the following classification: (1) the minor genres of Antiquity that lead to the *Satyricon* and to *The Golden Ass*; (2) Sophistic novels; (3) chivalric romances; (4) the Baroque novel; (5) the Pastoral novel; (6) *Prüfungsroman*; (7) *Bildungsroman*; (8) the (auto)biographical novel; (9) the Gothic novel; (10) the Sentimental novel; (11) minor medieval genres (fabliaux, etc.); (12) the picaresque novel; (13) the parodic novel; (14) the syncretic novel of the nineteenth century. This list does not claim to be exhaustive. As an aside to the discussion, Bakhtin evokes the properties of the (English) humanistic novel, which is missing from the enumeration.

The study of the chronotope is explicitly dedicated to the description of the various models that have dominated the history of the novel. Actually it stops at the Renaissance (with Rabelais), but it does put forth some indications about later subgenres. Here the list runs more or less as follows: (1) the Sophistic or Hellenistic novel; (2) the novel of adventures and everyday life (*Satyricon, The Golden Ass*); (3) the (auto)biographical novel, with further subdivisions: (a) Platonic types or rhetorical novel; (b) "energetic" biography in the style of Plutarch or "analytic" biography following Suetonius; etc.; (4) chivalric romance; (5) lesser genres of the Middle Ages and Renaissance; (6) the Rabelaisian novel; (7) the Idyllic novel and its progeny: (a) the regional novel; (b) Sternian and Goethian novel; (c) Rousseauist novel; (d) the family novel, the novel of generations. Some additional subgenres, such as the *Prüfungsroman*, the *Bildungsroman* or *Erziehungsroman*, are also mentioned but not discussed.

In the fragments of the book on the *Bildungsroman* which have reached us (fragments that evidence their author's maturity of thought, and thus make even more regrettable the loss of the final manuscript), there is a third, shorter and synthetic listing, based on another criterion: the mode of representation of the main character; nonetheless, categories encountered previously, can be recognized here:

A classification according to the principle of construction of the image of the main character: the travel novel; the novel of the hero's trials [*Prüfungsroman*]; the biographical (autobiographical) novel; the novel of learning [*Bildungsroman*] (22:188).

I won't go into the details of the descriptions of the subgenres thus advanced; they fall within the historians' area of competence. I shall limit myself to two broad comments. The first concerns the obviously open, nonstructured, character of these lists, which evidence Bakhtin's attachment to an "analytic history" in preference to a "systematic" one. It is significant that the search for a system becomes weaker with the passage of time. "Discourse on the Novel" (1934-1935) may have proposed still a weak form of systematization, with its distribution of genre into two stylistic lines, but no trace of it is left in the study on the chronotope (1937-1938). The various chronotopes are not classed in any way; the same applies to the modes of construction of the image of the character.

The second comment has to do with the total autonomy of these lists: there is indeed no cross-reference among them. This is not surprising, since the three lists are extremely close to each other, not only in outline, but in details. For example, whether the problematic under discussion be stylistic or structural, Wolfram von Eschenbach's *Parzival* stands apart from the subgenre of the "chivalric romance," to which it is, in principle, attached, and it comes closer to novels whose prototype is *The Golden Ass* (21:188 and 23:301). Or again: the advent of the second stylistic line (heterology *in praesentia*), as we saw, was correlated to the great geographic and astronomical discoveries; but the same is true of the predominance achieved, in the Renaissance, by a new chronotope (exemplified by the same works).

In his novel, Rabelais opens our eyes in a way to a universal and unlimited chronotope of human life. In this he was perfectly attuned to the nascent era of great cosmological and geographic discoveries (23:391).

At first, one could say that this remarkable coincidence is evidence of the validity of Bakhtin's work: having undertaken three completely independent investigations, he ends with the same result each time, each inquiry confirming the others. Actually matters are simpler, yet quite revealing of Bakhtin's conception. In fact, none of these inquiries *ends* up with a list of genres; the list was actually given beforehand. We have seen that Bakhtin does not deduce genres from an abstract principle, in the manner of Schelling or Hegel; he *finds* them. History has left in its wake a number of works that have regrouped, in history as well, according to a small number of models. That is an empirical given. And Bakhtin's work does not consist in the establishment of genres, but, having found them, in their submission to analysis (which can be stylistic as well as chronotopic, or related to the conception of man revealed in them). Bakhtin's practice thus confirms his attachment to "analytical history," and beyond, to his conception of literary studies as a part of history.

Chapter Seven
Philosophical Anthropology

Otherness and Psychic Life

I have reserved for this last chapter those ideas of Bakhtin that I value most and that, I believe, hold the key to his whole work; they constitute, in his own terms, his "philosophical anthropology." They recur in strikingly stable form throughout the course of his career, from his very last writings to a book recently published but actually the first to be written (probably between 1922 and 1924) that finally helps us understand Bakhtin's whole trajectory (it is a work of theoretical aesthetics and "moral philosophy," very abstract but rich in details, whose last chapter has never been written whereas the first has been lost). These ideas have to do with otherness.

Bakhtin, then, comes across the problem at the very beginnings of his career, when he attempts to elaborate a coherent aesthetic theory, and, more specifically, a description of the creative act. To do so, he sees himself forced to posit a general conception of human existence, where the *other* plays a decisive role. This is then the fundamental principle: it is impossible to conceive of any being outside of the relations that link it to the other.

In life, we do this at every moment: we appraise ourselves from the point of view of others, we attempt to understand the transgredient moments of our very consciousness and to take them into account through the other. . . ; in a word, constantly and intensely, we oversee and apprehend the reflections of our life in the plane of consciousness of other men (3:16-17).

94

A term here requires particular attention: "transgredient." As with so many concepts he finds essential, Bakhtin borrows the term from German aesthetic thought (specifically from Jonas Cohen, *Allgemeine Ästhetik*, Leipzig, 1901); he uses it in complementary sense to "ingredients," to designate elements of consciousness that are external to it but nonetheless absolutely necessary for its completion, for its achievement of totalization. We shall see that this notion will have a primary importance.

More concretely, what is the role of the other in the accomplishment of individual consciousness? Bakhtin starts from the simplest ground: we can never see ourselves as a whole; the *other* is necessary to accomplish, even if temporarily, a perception of the self that the individual can achieve only partially with respect to himself. Possible objections to this postulate are examined at length: isn't a complete vision of the self possible in a mirror? Or, in the case of a painter, through the self-portrait? In both instances, the answer is: no.

When it [seeing oneself from the outside] succeeds, what is striking, in our external image, is a sort of strange *void*, its *ghostlike* character, and its somewhat *sinister* loneliness. How to account for this impression? Thusly: we do not have, toward this image, an affective or volitional outlook, that could animate it and, by valorizing it, integrate it into the external unity of the plastic and pictural world (3:29). In any case, it seems to me that it is always possible to tell a self-portrait from a portrait, by the somewhat *ghostly* character taken on by the face in the first; the self-portrait, in a way, does not encompass the complete man, not wholly and absolutely: Rembrandt's laughing face in his self-portrait always leaves me with a sinister feeling (3:22).

The image I see in the mirror is necessarily incomplete; yet, in a way, it provides us with the archetype of self-perception; only someone else's gaze can give me the feeling that I form a totality.

I cannot perceive myself in my external aspect, feel that it encompasses me and gives me expression. . . . In this sense, one can speak of the absolute aesthetic need of man for the other, for the other's activity of seeing, holding, putting together and unifying, which alone can bring into being the externally finished personality; if someone else does not do it, this personality will have no existence (3:33-34).

Conversely, our own idea (or perhaps illusion) of what is a whole person, an accomplished being, can only come from the perception of someone else, and not from the perception we have of ourselves.

It is only in another human being that I find an aesthetically (and ethically) convincing experience of human finitude, of a marked-off empirical objectivity (3:34). Only another human being can give me the appearance of being consubstantial with the external world (3:38). For only the other can be embraced, totally surrounded, and explored lovingly in all of his or her limits (3:39).

It is not only the external apprehension of the body that needs the other's gaze; our apprehension of our internal selves is also seamlessly bound to someone else's perception, as evidenced by the way in which the small child discovers its body by naming its parts with borrowings from the "baby talk" of the father or the mother. "In this sense, the body is not a self-sufficient entity; it needs the *other,* his recognition and his formative activity" (3:47).

It is remarkable that these ideas, so close to the teachings of contemporary psychoanalysis, remain absolutely unchanged when, nearly fifty years later, Bakhtin returns to this issue.

All that touches me comes to my consciousness—beginning with my name—from the outside world, passing through the mouths of others (from the mother, etc.), with their intonation, their affective tonality, and their values. At first I am conscious of myself only through others: they give me the words, the forms, and the tonality that constitute my first image of myself. . . . Just as the body is initially formed in the womb of the mother (in her body), so human consciousness awakens surrounded by the consciousness of others (38:42).

And in the project to revise the *Dostoevsky:*

I achieve self-consciousness, I become myself only by revealing myself to another, through another and with another's help. The most important acts, constitutive of self-consciousness, are determined by their relation to another consiousness (a "thou"). Cutting oneself off, isolating oneself, closing oneself off, those are the basic reasons for loss of self. . . . It turns out that every internal experience occurs on the border, it comes across another, and this essence resides in this intense encounter. . . . The very being of man (both internal and external) is a *profound communication. To be* means to *communicate.* . . . To be means to be for the other, and through him, for oneself. Man has no internal sovereign territory; he is all and always on the boundary; looking within himself, he looks *in the eyes of the other* or *through the eyes of the other.* . . . I cannot do without the other; I cannot become myself without the other; I must find myself in the other, finding the other in me (in mutual reflection and perception). Justification cannot be justification of *oneself,* confession cannot be confession of *oneself.* I receive my name from the other, and this name exists for the other (to name oneself is to engage in usurpation). Self-love is equally impossible (31:311-12).

Whoever wants to preserve himself, loses himself; internally we are all boundaries; and in "being" (être) we should read: the other (autre). It is clear now why Bakhtin attaches so much importance to dialogue. "Life is dialogical by its very nature. To live means to engage in dialogue, to question, to listen, to answer, to agree, etc." (31:318).

These theses may be broadened: not only does being become human only through the action of the other, but the whole world is no longer what it was as soon as the first consciousness emerges.

Witness and judge. As soon as consciousness appears in the world (in being), perhaps even as soon as biological life appears (perhaps not only animals but even trees and grass witness and judge), the world (being) changes radically. The stone remains stone and the sun remains sun, but the event of being in its (unattainable) whole becomes altogether other because, on the stage of earthly being, for the first time, a new and decisive character in the event makes his entrance: the witness and the judge. And the sun, which retains its physical identity, becomes other, through the act of consciousness that the witness and judge have of it. It has ceased just being, to begin to be in itself and for itself (these categories appear for the first time) and for the other, because it is reflected in the consciousness of another (witness and judge): in this, it has changed radically, because richer and transformed (38:341).

A misprision must, however, be avoided in interpreting the importance of the other as resting on a parallelism between the other and the self; "I" and "thou" are radically distinct, asymmetrical: the difference is correlative to the need of the other (it could be said that this is the most insistent point of the early book). Bakhtin reverses the Christian injunction "love your neighbor as yourself":

One can feel the other's love for oneself, one can want to be loved, one can imagine and anticipate the other's love, but one cannot love oneself as one loves another, unmediatedly. . . . One cannot love one's neighbor as one loves oneself, or, more precisely, one cannot *love oneself* as if one were one's neighbor. . . . Suffering, the fear for oneself, joy, all are qualitatively and deeply different from compassion, the fear for the other, common joy; that is why there is a difference of principle in the moral qualifications of these feelings (3:44-45).

The objectivation of the I, the erasure of its pseudosingularity can be attained only after long efforts.

I hides in the *other* and in *others*; it wants to be but another for others, to fully penetrate the world of others as another, and heave aside the weight of an *I* unique in the word (the *I-for-myself*) (38:352).

The morphological parallelism of the pronouns—"mine," "yours," "his"—leads us to a false analogy between entities that are radically distinct and irreducible: "my love" and "his love," "my life" and "his life," "my death" and "his death."

In the life that I experience from within, I cannot, in principle, live the events of my birth and my death; to the extent that they are *mine*, they cannot become events in my own life. . . . The events of my birth, of my valorized being-in-the-world, and finally of my death are not accomplished in me or for me. The affective weight of my life *as a whole* does not exist for me. Only the other is in possession of the values of the being of a given person (3:42-93).

I can die only for others; conversely, for me, only others die; as Bakhtin puts it in passing "in all the cemeteries there are only others" (3:99). And he writes in 1961:

Man, life, destiny, have a beginning and an end, a birth and a death; but not consciousness, which is infinite by its very nature, since it can reveal itself only from the inside, that is for consciousness itself. Beginning and end take place in an objective (and objectal) universe for others, but not for the consciousness involved. It is not a case of not seeing death from the inside, by analogy with the fact that we cannot see the back of our neck without a mirror. The back of the neck exists objectively and others can see it. But there exists no death from the inside; it exists for no one, not for the dying, nor for others; it has absolutely no existence (31:315). The absence of a conscious death (death-for-oneself) is as objective a fact as the absence of conscious birth. Therein resides the specificity of consciousness (31:316).[1]

Otherness and Artistic Creation

Such are the broad lines of Bakhtin's conception of the human person. This conception, as soon as it arises, is no longer a goal in itself; it is simply necessary to shore up his theory of the creative act. Bakhtin's thinking seems to rely here on a German aesthetician of the period, W. Worringer (who, in turn, summarizes and synthesizes Riegl, Lipps, etc.). For Worringer, creative activity is a *Selbstentäusserung*, a dispossession of the self, a loss of the self in the external world: art is born only at the moment that the artist gives objective reality to his artistic will.

Aesthetic pleasure is objectivized pleasure of the self. To experience aesthetic pleasure is to have pleasure of oneself in a sense object, distinct of oneself; it is to be in empathy (*Einfühlung*) with it.[2]

More exactly, this dispossession has two variants: empathy or identification (individual tendency), and abstraction (universal tendency).

From this scheme, Bakhtin takes the idea of exit from the self: in literature, for example, the novelist creates a character materially distinct from himself; but rather than posit two *variants* of this activity (empathy and abstraction), Bakhtin asserts the necessity of distinguishing between two stages in *every* creative act: first, the stage of empathy or identification (the novelist puts himself in the place of his character), then a reverse movement whereby the novelist returns to his own position. This second aspect of creative activity is named by Bakhtin with a new Russian coinage: *vnenakhodimost'*, literally "finding oneself outside," which I shall translate, again literally, but with a Greek root, as *exotopy*.

The first moment of aesthetic activity is identification [*vzhivanie*]: I must experience, i.e., see and know, what he experiences, put myself in his place, in a way coincide with him. . . . But is this plenitude of internal fusion the ultimate end of aesthetic activity? . . . Not at all: properly speaking, aesthetic activity has not even begun. . . . Aesthetic activity begins properly only when one returns within oneself at one's place, outside of the one suffering, and when one gives form and completion to the material of identification (3:24-26).

We now know why this double movement is necessary: the author can accomplish, achieve, and close off his character only if he is external to him; he is the other bearing the transgredient elements that the character needs in order to be complete (conversely the expression of self in art is impossible; only a relation to the other can be expressed).

Only the other as such can be the axiological center of the artistic vision, and therefore, a character of the work; only the other can be essentially formed and finished, because all the aspects of axiological completion—spatial, temporal, or semantic—are transgredient in relation to active self-consciousness. . . . *I* is, aesthetically, unreal for itself. . . . In all aesthetic forms, the organizing force is the axiological category of the other, the relation to the other, enriched with the axiological surplus of the vision to reach a transgredient completion (3:163-64).

Aesthetic events are therefore irreducible to the one.

There are events that, in principle, cannot unfold on the plane of a single and unified consciousness, but presuppose two consciousnesses that do not fuse;

they are events whose essential and constitutive element is the relation of a consciousness to *another* consciousness, precisely because it is *other*. Such are all events that are creatively productive, innovative, unique, and irreversible (3:77-78). All the characteristics and definitions of present being that launch this being into dramatic movement, from the naive anthropocentrism of myth (cosmogony, theogony) all the way to the devices of contemporary art and the categories of aesthetizing intuitive philosophy, burn from the borrowed light of *alterity* (*drugosti*): beginning and end, birth and annihilation, being and becoming, life, etc. (3:118).

In a text from roughly the same period (1924), Bakhtin comes across the same problem.

The artist does not get involved in the event as a direct participant—in such a case, he would be a knowing subject, acting in the ethical sphere; instead, he occupies an essential position outside the event as disinterested viewer but *with an understanding of the axiological meaning of what is happening*; he does not experience it, but coexperiences it, since the event cannot be viewed as such unless, in some measure, we participate in it by evaluating it. This exotopy (which is not indifference) allows artistic activity to give the event unity, form, and completion *from outside*. Such a unification and such a completion are radically impossible from inside this knowledge and from inside this act (4:33).

Two remarks need be made here. The first is that there is a point of uncertainty in Bakhtin's conception at this time. We have seen him assert that the author must, in a way, return to his place, after an initial empathy for his character; yet, a few pages earlier, he seemed to have thought the opposite:

In the aesthetic self-objectivation of person-author within a character, one must return to the self: the entity of the characters must remain a final totality for the other-author (3:17).

A second uncertainty is even greater (it is not unrelated to the first): it would be possible to make a distinction between two theses in the hypothetical reconstruction of the creative act put forward by Bakhtin. If one is concerned with the necessary alterity and exotopy, the other is concerned with transgredience: the character must be a completed whole, and the author is the one to give him the necessary elements for this completion. The author is the externality that makes it possible for the character to be seen as a whole; the author is the consciousness that wholly encompasses the character, the unity with respect to which we measure the difference among characters. But those are two judgments of a different nature: the first takes cognizance of the given; it aims at being descriptive; the second tells how to proceed and what realization is better; it is a prescriptive statement.

Yet, in this early text, the two judgments are always co-present, even if their author sees them as distinct, since he describes instances where the relation of transgredience is not perfectly realized. Bakhtin even outlines a typologic of these diseases of transgredience, the first instance of which involves an overflow of the characters on the author ("the character grabs hold of the author," 3:18) and, by means of illustration, he adds: "almost all of Dostoevsky's characters belong to this type" (3:20). The condemnation that Bakhtin then levels against this diseased transgredience is irrevocable.

The crisis of the author can take another course as well. The very position of exotopy turns out shaky and appears as inessential; the right of the author to stand outside life and to complete it is challenged. And there begins the disintegration of all stable transgredient forms (most of all in prose, from Dostoevsky to Biely, because the crisis of the author has a lesser significance for lyric poetry: cf. Annenski *et al.*): life then becomes understandable and takes on its full weight only from the inside, from where I experience it as an *I*, in the form of a relation to the self, in the valorized categories of my I-for-myself: to understand comes to mean to live the object from inside, to look at it with its own eyes, to renounce the essentiality of exotopy in relation to it (3:176).

And also:

The exotopy becomes morbid and ethical (the humiliated and the offended become, in this capacity of theirs, the character of a vision, that is no longer purely artistic, of course). The assured, calm, unshakable, and rich position of exotopy is no more (3:178).

What Bakhtin censures Dostoevsky for here is to have questioned transgredient exotopy, the stability, the reassuring character of authorial consciousness, that made it possible for the reader to always know where the truth lay.

In a text signed Voloshinov and published a few years later, this disintegration of the stable ideological framework—no longer attributed to Dostoevsky alone—becomes part of a Marxist discourse condemning contemporary bourgeois ideology; it is the last page of *Marxism and the Philosophy of Language*, which deserves to be quoted in full.

The markers of the subject, whether typical or individual, in the utterance have achieved such an autonomy in linguistic consciousness that they have completely occulted and relativized its semantic kernel: the responsible social perspective that is expressed in it. It is as if the semantic content of the utterance were no longer taken seriously. *Categorical* discourse, *responsible* discourse, *assertatory* discourse, survive only in scientific contexts. In all other realms of verbal creation, "fictive" discourse dominates, not "uttered" discourse. All verbal activity is reduced to the allocation of "someone else's discourse" and "the seemingly someone else's discourse." Even in the human sciences, there has arisen a tendency to replace responsible utterance by an exposition of the present state of research and by the evocation of "dominant viewpoint these days," sometimes taken to be the safest "solution" to the problem. All of this reveals the astonishing instability and uncertainty of ideological discourse. Literary discourse and rhetorical discourse, that of philosophy and that of the human sciences, have become the realms of "opinions," notorious opinions, and even in these opinions, front stage is not given to the *what*, but to the *how* — the individual or typical manner in which this opinion is arrived at. This turn in the destiny of discourse in bourgeois Western Europe as well as among us (almost until today) can be defined as the *reification of discourse*, as the deterioration of the semantic dimension of discourse (12:157).

It could be said that what this page denounces is the generalization of cited discourse at the expense of a discourse fully assumed by its subject.

Let us note here, in anticipation of what follows, that Bakhtin, at the end of his life, finds again the same characteristics in modernity, but, this time, he modifies his evaluation.

Irony has entered into all the languages of modern times (especially into French); it has introduced itself in all the words and all the forms. . . . Man in modern times does not declaim but he speaks, that is, he speaks within restrictions. Declamatory genres are essentially preserved as parodic or semi-parodic ingredients of the novel. . . . The uttering subjects of high declamatory genres — priests, prophets, preachers, judges, leaders, fathers-patriarchs, etc. — have left life. They have been replaced by the writer, the simple writer, who inherited their styles (38:336). The author's search for a discourse that would be his own basically is part of the search for genre and style, for the position of the author. That is now the most acute problem of contemporary literature, that has led many authors to give up the genre of the novel and to replace it by montage of documents, by the description of objects; it ultimately leads them to concrete literature and, in some measure, to literature of the absurd. All of this could be defined, in a sense, as different forms of silence. These searches have led Dostoevsky to the creation of the polyphonic novel. Dostoevsky was not able to find a discourse for a monologic novel. Parallel itinerary for Tolstoy toward popular tales (primitivism), toward the introduction of Gospel quotations (in concluding sections). Another way: force the world to speak and listen to the words of the world itself (Heidegger) (38:354).

As far as the relation of transgredience to modern writing is concerned, the juvenilia material from which I have extracted Bakhtin's theory of alterity may be unfinished, but in the first chapter it does offer the following project: "Finally we will verify our conclusions by an analysis of the relation of the author to characters in the works of Dostoevsky, Pushkin, and others" (3:7).

This project will never reach fruition. A few years later, however, in 1929, there appears the first publication signed by Bakhtin: the book on Dostoevsky. A radical transformation has already taken place between, let us say, 1924 and 1928: Bakhtin has reversed the direction of his "prescriptive" statement and he now espouses Dostoevsky's viewpoint. Far from "verifying" his initial theses by analyzing Dostoevsky's works, he has replaced them by their antitheses: now the best exotopy is precisely the one Dostoevsky practices, insofar as it does not confine the character in the consciousness of the author and puts into question the very notion of the privileging of one consciousness above another. A character in Dostoevsky is an unaccomplished, incomplete, heterogeneous being, but that is the reason of its superiority, because we are, all of us, as we have seen, subjects only in unaccomplishment. Basically, before Dostoevsky, literary characters were ersatz beings, granted a reassuring transgredience by an accommodating author; Dostoevsky's characters are like us; that is, incomplete, they are like so many *authors*, rather than the characters of ancient authors.

Bakhtin does rely on previous critics in this interpretation of Dostoevsky, but he systematically exceeds their assertions. For example, Grossman wrote in 1925:

In spite of the immemorial traditions of aesthetics, that require a correspondence between a matter and its elaboration, that presuppose the unity, and, in any case, the homogeneity and the relatedness of the constructive elements of a given artistic creation, Dostoevsky brings contraries into fusion (quoted in 13:21-22 and 32:18-19).

Bakhtin takes up this assertion but gives it a more radical meaning. Nurtured in the spirit of Romantic aesthetics, Grossman conceives of all difference in terms of opposition; but, as soon as two contraries have been posited, their fusion can be anticipated. Bakhtin, for his part, insists on the *heterogeneous* nature of Dostoevsky's characters.

To anyone who sees and understands the represented world in exclusively monologic fashion, to anyone who evaluates the construction of the novel in accordance with the monologic canon, to such a person, Dostoevsky's universe may seem a chaos, and the construction of his novels, a monstrous assemblage of the most heterogeneous matters and the most incompatible principles of form-giving

(13:11; cf. 32:4). Racine's hero is equal to himself, Dostoevsky's hero does not coincide for a moment with himself (32:68).

Bakhtin will even explicitly oppose any attempt to reabsorb Dostoevsky's scatter by means of the Hegelian dialectical scheme as had been proposed by Engelgardt, another precursor of his.

The unique spirit in its dialectical becoming, understood in Hegel's sense, can only generate a philosophical monologue. Monist Idealism is the least favorable ground for the flowering of a multiplicity of unmerged consciousnesses. Even as image, the unique spirit in becoming is organically foreign to Dostoevsky. Dostoevsky's world is deeply *pluralistic* (13:41-42 and 32:36).

Bakhtin will always prove quite suspicious of Hegelian dialectics, in any case, taking exception to its desire of unifying everything—he refers to it as "Hegel's monological dialectic," and he speaks of the "monologism of Hegel's *Phenomenology of Spirit*" (40:364); on another occasion, he defines the difference between dialectic and dialogue thus:

Dialogue and dialectics. Season the words of a dialogue (the division of voices); season then the intonations (of a personal and affective character); shell abstract notions and reasonings from live words and sayings; wrap the whole in a unique abstract consciousness—and you get dialectics.

Instead of a "dialectics of nature" Bakhtin puts forward a "dialogics of culture."

The renunciation of the unity of the "I" has its counterpart in the assertion of a new status for the "thou" of the other. The poet Viacheslav Ivanov (not to be confused with the semiotician) characterized Dostoevsky's contribution in these terms: "To affirm the self of the other not as an object but as another subject, 'you are'" (13:14 and 32:12). Bakhtin will amplify and nuance this idea throughout his book.

Here [in Dostoevsky's novels], we don't have a great number of destinies and lives developing within a single objective world, enlightened by the consciousness of the author alone; rather we have a *plurality of consciousnesses, with equal rights, each with its own world*, combining in the unity of an event but nonetheless without fusing. . . . The character's consciousness is given as another consciousness, as belonging to someone else, without being reified in the least, or closed in, without having become the object of authorial consciousness. . . . In his works, there comes forward a character whose voice is constructed in the same way as the voice of an author is in an ordinary novel, not that of a character. The discourse of a character about himself and about the world has the same weight as the discourse of an ordinary author; it is beholden to the objectal image of the character, like one of its features; nor is he used as the author's mouthpiece. He enjoys an exceptional degree of independence in the structure of the work; in a way, he sounds off alongside authorial discourse, and, in specific fashion, enters into combination with it and with the equally qualified voices of other characters. . . . The position from which a narrative can be unfolded, a representation constructed, or information given, must be set in a new mode in relation to this new world—not a world of objects but of subjects vested with full rights (13:8-10; cf. 7-8).

Or more briefly, in 1961:

This consciousness of the other is not framed by authorial consciousness, it reveals itself from inside as standing *outside* and *beside*, and the author enters into dialogical relations with it. Like Prometheus, the author creates (more precisely, recreates) living beings independent of himself, with whom he appears to be on an equal footing (31:309).[3]

In granting authorial discourse exceptional status, writers prior to Dostoevsky wanted to make us believe in the possibility of a single position: the characters needed the author to achieve completion, but the author, for his part, held a position that needed no complement. Yet, this peculiarity is not only simply regrettable, it does not exist, and that is the essential point. All that exists is a conception of being that asserts that its natural state is to be alone and independent of anyone else; this individualistic and Romantic conception is the product of a state of capitalist or bourgeois society (but the socialist ideal, it could be added, is but its culmination).

In this, Dostoevsky is opposed to all decadent and idealist (individualistic) culture, to the culture of principled and desperate loneliness. He asserts the impossibility of solitude, the illusory character of solitude. . . . Capitalism has created the conditions for a specific type of desperate and lonely consciousness. Dostoevsky unveils all the lie of this consciousness, which is caught in a vicious circle. . . . No *human* event unfolds or is decided within a single consciousness. Hence Dostoevsky's hostility toward those conceptions of the world that see the ultimate end in a fusion, in the dissolution of consciousness into a single consciousness, in the sublation of individuation. . . . After Dostoevsky . . . there appeared the role of the *other*, in whose light every discourse on the self constructs itself (31:312-14).

Artistic completion and perfection are then, on the whole, but a subtle form of violence done to the individual to present him as self-sufficient.

Critique to all *external* forms of the relation to, and action upon, the other: from violence to authority; artistic completion as a variant of violence (31:317).

The term *exotopy* recovers here its full meaning: not a transgredient exteriority, used to encompass the other, but an elsewhere beyond integration or reduction.

No fusion with the other but the preservation of his *exotopic* position and of his *excess* of vision and comprehension, that is its correlative. But the question arises as to how Dostoevsky uses this surplus. Not for objectivation of completion. The most important moment of this surplus is love (one cannot love oneself, it is a coordinated relation); then, confession, forgiveness (the conversation between Stavrogin and Tikhon), finally, simply an active understanding (that does not reduplicate), watchful listening [*uslyshannost'*] (31:324-25).

There have been frequent misprisions of Bakhtin's interpretation of Dostoevsky; the notion that, in Dostoevsky, all positions are equally valid, the author having no opinion of his own, has been attributed to him. Such is not the case; in these novels, characters can enter in a *dialogue* with the author: the structure of the relation is what is different, not its content.

Our point of view is not at all tantamount to asserting a kind of passivity on the part of the author, who would confine himself to making a montage of the viewpoints of others, of the truths of others, and would surrender altogether his own viewpoint, his truth. That is not at all the case; rather it is a case of an entirely new and specific interrelation between his truth and the truth of someone else. The author is profoundly *active*, but his action takes on a specific *dialogic* character. . . . Dostoevsky frequently interrupts the other's voice but he does not cover it up, he never finishes it from the "self," that is from an alien consciousness (his own) (31:310).

It could even be said that Dostoevsky, finding the exceptional position in which he has put himself impossible to bear, sometimes aspires to the mediocre condition of the average Joe who expresses himself through his own voice; he succeeds in this in his journalistic writings (*Diary of a Writer*).

In search of one's own voice (belonging to the author). To incarnate oneself, to become more determined, to become lesser, more limited, more stupid. Not to remain on the tangent, penetrate into the circle of life, become one among men. To reject restrictions, reject irony (38:352). When we enter into the realm of Dostoevsky's journalistic writings, one observes a sudden narrowing of the horizon; the novel's universality gives way, even though the problem of the intimate lives of the characters have been replaced by social and political problems (38:357).

It was not really possible, as we have seen, to maintain a distinction between a discourse of dialogical nature and a monologic discourse, since every discourse is, by its very nature, "dialogical," that is, caught in intertextual relations. On the other hand, the opposition recovers its oppositeness as soon as it is invoked in the field of theories of discourse, or of consciousness.

Ultimately, *monologism* denies that there exists outside of it another consiousness, with the same rights, and capable of responding on an equal footing, another and equal *I (thou)*. For a monologic outlook (in its extreme or pure form) the *other* remains entirely and only an *object* of consciousness, and cannot constitute another consciousness. No response capable of altering everything in the world of my consciousness, is expected of this other. The monologue is accomplished and deaf to the other's response; it does not await it and does not grant it any *decisive* force. Monologue makes do without the other; that is why to some extent it objectivizes all reality. Monologue pretends to be the *last word* (31:318).

We are witnessing here a singular metamorphosis: Dostoevsky has ceased standing as the object of the study undertaken by Bakhtin to pass to the very side of the subject: he is the one who has taught Bakhtin his new position, and all the theoretical and practical work that Bakhtin will dedicate himself to from this moment onward, appears henceforth as merely the application and interpretation of Dostoevsky's teaching: it is Dostoevsky, and not Bakhtin who has invented intertextuality! But isn't it the essential characteristic of knowledge in the human sciences, as Bakhtin describes it, not to deal with the mute "object" of the natural sciences, and to transform itself into a dialogue of texts, knowing and to be known?[4]

Alterity and Interpretation

Artistic creation cannot be analyzed outside of a theory of alterity: which means also that to produce is to understand. It will not be surprising then to see Bakhtin, in some of his last writings, turn toward the reception of texts and describe it in the same terms.

It could be said that there are three kinds of interpretation, just as there are, if Blanchot (in *L'Entretien Infini*) is to be believed, three kinds of human relations. The first consists in unifying in the name of the self: the critic projects himself in the work he reads, and all authors illustrate or exemplify his thought. The second kind corresponds to the "criticism of identification" (a denomination still assumed). The critic has no proper identity, there is but one identity, that of the author under examination, and the critic becomes his mouthpiece; we witness a kind of ecstatic fusion, and therefore once again we have unification. The third kind would be the dialogue advocated by Bakhtin, where each of the two identities remains affirmed (there is neither integration nor identification), where knowledge takes the form of a dialogue with a "thou" equal to the "I" and yet different from it. As with creation, Bakhtin gives empathy, or identification, merely a preparative, transitory role.

From his earliest writings, Bakhtin has been critical of the aesthetics, and the epistemology, of identification.

In what way will the event be enriched if I succeed in fusing with the other? If instead of two, there is now just one? What do *I* gain by having the other fuse with me? He will know and see but what I know and see, he will but repeat within himself the tragic dimension of my life. Let him rather stay on the outside because from there he can know and see what I cannot see or know from my vantage point, and he can thus enrich essentially the event of my life. In a *mere* fusion with someone else's life, I only deepen its tragic character, literally double it (3:78).

If this road of illusion has been followed, where understanding is reduced to identification, it is because all cognition has been conceived of in the image of cognition in the natural sciences, which, as we have seen, deal with objects and not with other subjects, and know of only one consciousness: that of the scientist himself. Interpreters of culture have had recourse to the same model, whereas they should, quite to the contrary, have recognized and maintained the constitutive duality of their activity, the only source of enrichment.

If there are two of us, what matters from the point of view of the actual productivity of the event is not that alongside of me there is *yet one more* man, essentially *similar* to me (*two men*) but that he is, for me, an *other* man. In this way, his simple sympathy for my life is not tantamount to our fusing into a single being and it does not constitute a numerical duplication of any life, but an essential enrichment of the event. Because the other co-experiences my life in a new form, as the life of an other man, perceived and valorized otherwise, and justified in a way other than his life. The productivity of the event does not lie in the fusion of all into one, but in the tension of my exotopy and my nonfusion, in the reliance upon the privilege afforded me by my unique position, outside other men (3:78-79).

At the end of his life, Bakhtin returns to these themes to denounce once again the temptation of unity in relation to understanding.

Penetration in someone else (fusion with him) and the keeping of the distance (of his place), that insures the excess of cognition (28:410). The mistaken tendency to reduce everything to a single consciousness, to dissolve in it the other's consciousness (that one understands). The advantages, in principle, of exotopy (spatial, temporal, national). Understanding cannot be understood as empathy [*vchustvovanie*] and setting of the self in another place (loss of one's place). That is required only of the marginal aspects of understanding. Understanding cannot be understood as the translation of a foreign language into one's tongue (38:346). Understanding as the transformation of the other into a "self-other." The principle of exotopy (4):371).

That is why it is no longer enough to understand a text as its author did (as positivistic hermeneutics believes). The author is always partially unconscious with respect to his work, and the subject of understanding is obligated to enrich the meaning of the text; he is equally creative.

Understanding could also be presented as composed of two stages.

The first task is to understand the work as the author understood it, without leaving the limits of his understanding. The accomplishment of this task is most demanding and usually requires the scrutiny of an immense corpus.
The second task is to use one's temporal and cultural exotopy. Inclusion in our context (alien to the author) (38:349).

Understanding is not considered then only as an interpersonal process but also as a relation between two cultures; identification, or empathy, has only a transitory, preparatory role.

There is an enduring image, that is partial, and therefore false, according to which to better understand a foreign culture one should live in it, and, forgetting one's own, look at the world through the eyes of this culture. As I have said, such an image is partial. To be sure, to enter in some measure into an alien culture and look at the world through its eyes, is a necessary moment in the process of its understanding; but if understanding were exhausted in this moment, it would have been no more than a single duplication, and would have brought nothing new or enriching. *Creative understanding* does not renounce its self, its place in time, its culture; it does not forget anything. The chief matter of understanding is the *exotopy* of the one who does the understanding—in time, space, and culture—in relation to that which he wants to understand creatively. Even his own external aspect is not really accessible to man, and he cannot interpret it as a whole; mirrors and photographs prove of no help; a man's real external aspect can be seen and understood only by other persons, thanks to their spatial exotopy, and thanks to the fact that they are *other*.
In the realm of culture, exotopy is the most powerful lever of understanding. It is only to the eyes of an *other* culture that the alien culture reveals itself more

completely and more deeply (but never exhaustively, because there will come other cultures, that will see and understand even more) (36:334).

To read these lines, it would seem that Bakhtin is intent in imposing to all reading, all cognition, the status of ethnology, the discipline that defines itself by the exotopy of its researcher in relation to his object—at the same time that he is grounding, better than the ethnologists themselves, the legitimacy of their discipline. This does not appear to me to be a reformulation of the well-known "hermeneutic circle," where, through successive approximations, one sets oneself up in the object of knowledge, but rather a matter of preserving the difference between two texts. It is for this precise reason that the meaning we identify in a text is never final, and that interpretation is infinite. (The following written fragment is the last written by Bakhtin, in 1974).

There is no first or last discourse, and dialogical context knows no limits (it disappears into an unlimited past and in our unlimited future). Even *past* meanings, that is those that have arisen in the dialogue of past centuries, can never be stable (completed once and for all, finished), they will always change (renewing themselves) in the course of the dialogue's subsequent development, and yet to come. At every moment of the dialogue, there are immense and unlimited masses of forgotten meanings, but, in some subsequent moments, as the dialogue moves forward, they will return to memory and live in renewed form (in a new context). Nothing is absolutely dead: every meaning will celebrate its rebirth. The problem of the *great temporality* (40:373).

A last complement: even if there is no ideal reader, who could totalize the meaning of a text, the author can still dream of it; in fact, to understand the strategy of writing it is necessary to identify this "super-recipient" imagined by the author. Bakhtin has devoted to this question a few pages not exempt of emotion, in an unpublished text dating probably from 1961:

Every utterance always has a receiver (of different nature; different degrees of proximity, specificity, consciousness, etc.) whose responsive understanding is sought and anticipated by the author of the verbal work. He is a "second" (in a nonarithmetical sense). But, in addition to this receiver (the "second") the author imagines, more or less consciously, a higher *super-receiver* (a third) whose absolutely appropriate responsive understanding is projected either into a metaphysical distance or into a distant historical time. (A spare receiver.) In different periods and in different conceptions of the world, such super-receivers and their (ideally appropriate) responsive understanding receive various concrete ideological expressions (God, the absolute truth, the fragment, impartial human conscience, the people, the judgment of history, science, etc.). The author can never totally surrender both himself and his verbal work to the complete and definitive will of present or near-by recipients (proximate descendants can err as well) and so he imagines . . . (more or less consciously) a sort of higher instance of responsive understanding, that can recede in various directions. Every dialogue takes place then, in a way, against the backdrop of the responsive understanding of a present but invisible third entity, hovering above all the participants in the dialogue (the partners). (Cf. the understanding of the Fascist jail or of "hell" in Thomas Mann as an absolute *lack* of *watchful listening*, as the absolute absence of a *third person* [Reference to *Doctor Faustus*, chapter 25].) The "third" in question is nowise a mystical or metaphysical entity (even if, though in some conceptions of the world, it does receive such status); it is a constitutive moment of the whole utterance, that a penetrating analysis can bring to light. It proceeds from the nature of discourse, that always wants to be heard, that always is in search of responsive understanding, and does not stop at *the most proximate understanding* but makes its way further and further away (without limits). For discourse (and, therefore, for man) nothing is more frightening than the *absence of answer* (30:305-6).

One does not feel the right to confine oneself to pure textual analysis here, and to forget the circumstances in which these very pages were written. Some have relished in pointing out the paradox of having an invalid and mutilated individual write the paean to the body that is the *Rabelais*. But isn't it even more moving to see the theoretician of dialogue, a man for whom the absence of response is evil absolute, hell, suffer this singular fate: never get a response? Either his books appear, but under another name; then someone else gets the response (we have a letter full of astonishment from Pasternak addressed to Medvedev: Pasternak did not imagine him capable of such penetration); or he takes the responsibility for his books, but to put them in a drawer: twenty-five years for the *Rabelais*, forty for *Questions of Literature and Aesthetics*; and a book written before 1925 will appear only toward 1980 . . . ; others may never appear, lost or censored. At a time of frenzied overpublication, one can admire Bakhtin's determination for developing the same thoughts over fifty years while putting them away in his files. But one may well wonder to what extent the whole theory of dialogue may have originated from the desire to understand this unbearable state—the absence of response. Bakhtin describes the fate of Dostoevsky's characters in capitalistic society thus:

Hence the representation of sufferings, humiliations, and the nonrecognition of man in class-society. His recognition and his name have been taken away. He has been thrown out into forced loneliness, that the unsubjugated attempt to transform into *proud solitude* (making do without recognition, without others) (31:312).

What is there to say about his fate, in his society? And does it suffice to imagine super-receivers to compensate the absence of recipients, of responsive understanding? It is in order to remedy this lack that I have tried, in these pages, to have Bakhtin's voice be heard again: so that the dialogue can finally begin.

Notes

Notes

Introduction

1. I wish to thank here all those who have aided me in the writing of this book: Ladyslav Matejka, James M. Holquist, Georges Philippenko, and many other friends in the U.S.S.R. and Bulgaria, as well as Monique Canto.

Chapter One: Biography

1. V. V. Kozhinov, S. Konkin, "Mikhail Mikhailovich Bakhtin, Kratkij ocherk zhizni i dejatel'nosti," in *Problemy poétiki i istorii literatury* (Saransk, 1973), pp. 5-19, Hereinafter cited in the text as Kozhinov/Konkin.

2. For this period in Bakhtin's life, I rely upon the notes of K. Nevel'skaja which accompany her publication "M. M. Bakhtin i M. I. Kagan," *Pamjat* 4 (1981).

3. I understand that a new volume of unedited texts is in preparation in the U.S.S.R., under the direction of V. Kozhinov.

4. V. V. Ivanov, "Znachenie idej M. M. Bakhtina . . . ," *Trudy po znakovym systemam* VI (Tartu, 1973):44.

5. Russian text in V. Ivanov, "O Bakhtin i semiotike," *Rossija/Russia* 2 (Torino, 1975): 294.

6. Thomas G. Winner, "The Beginnings of Structural and Semiotic Aesthetics," in *Sound, Sign, and Meaning*, ed. L. Matejka, Michigan Slavic Contributions 6 (Ann Arbor, 1976), p. 451, n. 2.

7. Cf. A. J. Wehrle, "Introduction: M. M. Bakhtin/P. N. Medvedev," in P. N. Medvedev/ M. M. Bakhtin, *The Formal Method in Literary Scholarship* (Baltimore & London: The Johns Hopkins University Press, 1978).

8. This is the typographical solution adopted by A. Wehrle in his English translation of *The Formal Method in Literary Studies.*

115

Chapter Two: Epistemology of the Human Sciences

1. This sentence is in fact extracted from an article by S. S. Averintsev, "Simvol," published in volume six of the Soviet *Brief Literary Encyclopedia*, an article evoked by Bakhtin within these same pages.

Chapter Three: Major Options

1. It is tempting to compare these sentences, and others of the same sort that abound in Bakhtin's writings from these years, with the way the idea has been formulated, in a very different style, in Emmanuel Levinas, who was himself influenced by the existentialist current, with which Bakhtin's thought evidences notable affinities: "L'expression, avant d'être célébration de l'être, est une relation avec celui à qui j'exprime l'expression et dont la présence est déjà requise pour que mon geste culturel d'expression se produise" [Expression, before being a celebration of being, is a relation to whoever it is to whom I express the expression and whose presence is already required for my cultural gesture of expression to be produced] (*Humanisme de l'autre homme*, 1972, p. 46).

2. Reflections on the social nature of human existence has a long history, both inside and ouside the tradition of Marxist thought. It is neither possible nor useful to reproduce here those reflections in their entirety. I will be content to indicate some points of reference. Hegel writes in his *Philosophical Propaedeutic*: "Self-consciousness is real for itself only to the extent that it recognizes its reflection in other consciousnesses." Ludwig Feuerbach writes in his *Principles of the Philosophy to Come* (1843): "The individual does not contain in himself or herself the essence of human being, neither as a moral being nor as a thinking being. The essence of human being is contained only within the community, in the unity of person with person. . . ."

Among Bakhtin's contemporaries we can cite, on the one hand, some philosophers of religion. In his *Religion der Vernunft aus den Quellen des Judentums* (1919), Hermann Cohen (whose importance for Bakhtin and his circle is known) wrote that "only the *thou*, the discovery of the *thou*, leads me to consciousness of my *I*." And Martin Buber (with whom Bakhtin was acquainted and whose works he esteemed) wrote in 1938: "The individual is a fact of existence to the extent that he or she enters into a living relation with other individuals. . . . The fundamental fact of human existence is person with person" (M. Buber, *The Problem of Man*).

It is necessary, on the other hand, to point out the proximity in thought that exists between Bakhtin and a founder of social psychology in the United States like George Herbert Mead. Voloshinov/Bakhtin would definitely not have been acquainted with Mead's theses, since they were not published until the thirties, after the death of Mead; but he had already referred in a positive way to the new behavioral psychology. Mead wrote, for example, in a manner parallel to Bakhtin (in *Mind, Self, and Society*, which I cite from the 1977 collection *George Herbert Mead on Social Psychology*, ed. Anselm Strauss [Chicago: University of Chicago Press, 1964]): "Self-consciousness refers to the ability to call out in ourselves a set of definite responses which belong to the others of the group" (p. 277). And, for an affirmation of the social nature of humanity: "The self, as that which can be an object to itself, is essentially a social structure. . . . It is impossible to conceive of a self arising outside of social experience" (p. 204). "A person is a personality because he belongs to a community" (p. 226). "The origin and foundations of the self, like those of thinking, are social" (p. 228).

We can recall finally the lapidary phrase of Claude Lévi-Strauss: "Whoever says man says language, and whoever says language says society" (*Tristes Tropiques* [Paris: 10/18, 1955], p. 351).

Chapter Four: Theory of the Utterance

1. Cf. E. Benveniste, *Problèmes de linguistique générale II* (Paris: Gallimard, 1974), particularly the chapter "Sémiologie de la langue" (the text had been published in 1969).

2. French translation in R. Jakobson, *Essais de linguistique générale I* (Paris: Minuit, 1963), p. 213.

Chapter Five: Intertextuality

1. H. Wölfflin, *Principles of Art History* (New York: Dover, 1950), pp. 18-19.

Chapter Six: History of Literature

1. The references to Friedrich Schlegel are to the *Kritische Ausgabe* (abbreviated KA), followed by, first, the number of the volume and then that of the page or fragment; or to the *Literary Notebooks 1797-1801* (LN) (London, 1957), followed by the number of the fragment.

2. *Esthétique, La poésie*, French translation, vol. 1 (Paris: Aubier, 1965), pp. 128-29. Translation from the German by Linda Schulte-Sasse.

Chapter Seven: Philosophical Anthropology

1. Here one might again mention, much as it was done with regard to Bakhtin's social psychology in general, that he was neither the first nor the only one to emphasize the constitutive character that the I-thou relation has for individual existence (this is a specific determination in relation to his general theory about the social nature of human existence). Even the usage of the personal pronouns "I" and "thou" is wholly traditional. This idea has been a part of classical philosophy since the end of the eighteenth century. Jacobi wrote in 1785: "The I is impossible without the thou." Fichte, in 1797: "The individual's consciousness is necessarily accompanied by that of another, of a thou, and is possible only on that condition." W. von Humboldt in 1827: "To achieve his own thought, man aspires to a thou corresponding to his I." L. Feuerbach in 1843: "The true I is that which holds itself in the presence of a thou and which is itself a thou in the presence of another I." But the affirmation becomes particularly strong within existential philosophy (in the broad sense of the word), that is, for example, in Martin Buber, from whom I have borrowed all the preceding examples (see "The History of the Dialogical Principle," in M. Buber, *Between Man and Man* [New York: Macmillan, 1965]), and who himself writes (one formulation among others): "Living means being called out to." (*La Vie en dialogue* [Paris: Aubier, 1959], p. 115). One also finds in Buber the terms "philosophical anthropology" and "polyphony" used in a sense comparable to Bakhtin (see, for example, *ibid.*, p. 120). Or, regarding the love of self: "Kierkegaard himself knows what love is; thus he knows that there is no self-love that is not illusion (since the party who loves—and that is who is at stake—loves only the other and not essentially himself or herself. . . ." [ibid., p. 155]). But let us mention it once again: Bakhtin is acquainted with Buber and on occasion cites him (see 23:249); his friend Pumpianski wrote in a letter of 1926, after a reading of *I and Thou*: "M. Buber is talented" (43). Let us also mention the presence of this theme in Sartre, who devoted one third of *Being and Nothingness* (1943) to the "for-others" ("pour autrui"), and who sums up Heidegger's contribution to the problematic in this way: "In a word, I find that the transcendent relation to others is constitutive of my own being. The other is no longer primarily this or that individual existence I encounter in the world—and one that would not be indispensable for my own existence, since I existed before encountering it: that existence is the ex-centric

term contributing to the constitution of my being" ([Paris: Gallimard, 1943, 1979], p. 290). Sartre concludes in his own name: "I need others to grasp fully at the structures of my being; the for-itself refers to the for-others" (*ibid.*, p. 267). Finally, the theme is familiar in social psychology; thus Mead: "The selves can exist only in relations determined along with other selves" (*op. cit.*, p. 227).

As is common in these matters, it is not the idea that is new in Bakhtin, but the place that it occupies in his system of thought, and the consequences it leads to. At the same time it should be clear from what has been mentioned that the intellectual family closest to Bakhtin is not Marxism, but rather existentialism, in some of its forms; in this regard one might also call attention to the respectful references to Heidegger in the last writings of Bakhtin. It must be admitted that his existentialism isn't incompatible with a certain type of Marxism; nowhere else has an existential philosophy been seen to produce works of "translinguistics."

2. French translation, *Abstraction et Einfühlung* (Paris: Klincksieck, 1978). p. 43.

3. This opposition that consists of relating to others as to an object or as to another subject, borrowed by Bakhtin from Viacheslav Ivanov, is not without philosophical parallels, whether it be in utilizing the distinction between subject and object, or the distinction between the personal pronouns that oppose the relation between *I* and *it* to the relation between *I* and *thou*. Perhaps William James first employed the formula ("The universe is for us no longer a simple *it*, but a *thou*. . . ." *The Will to Believe*, 1897); but it has become celebrated since the book of M. Buber, *I and Thou* (1923), which develops the opposition of the two relations I-it and I-thou; Buber has frequently returned to this theme in his later writings (see, for example, *La Vie en dialogue, op. cit.*, p. 113-15, 124, 238-41, etc.)

4. This may explain the curious reaction of Bakhtin in an interview dating from the last years of his life: on learning that his book on Dostoevsky's poetics had been translated into many languages (twice into French!), he refrained from taking credit for its merit, but explained the fact by saying that the many translations were due to the contemporary popularity of Dostoevsky (see 37:196). In the West one may not have the impression that Bakhtin is read on account of Dostoevsky but because of Bakhtin! But, in fairness, the opposition isn't where one might think, and Bakhtin's reaction is perhaps not as displaced as it appears: he perceived himself as a spokesman for Dostoevsky.

Chronological List

Chronological List
of the Writings of Bakhtin
and His Circle

1. M. Bakhtin, "Iskusstvo i otvetstvennost" [Art and responsibility]. In (42), pp. 5-6. Earlier publication in: *Den' iskusstva* (1919) and in *Voprosy literatury* 6 (1977).

2. V. N. Voloshinov, "Recenzija na knigu I. Glebova o Chajkovskom" [Review of a book by I. Glebov on Tchaïkovski]. *Zapiski peredvizhnogo teatra* 42 (1922). With other texts by Voloshinov, Moussorgsky and Beethoven, published in the review *Iskusstvo.* Vitebsk, 1921.

3. M. Bakhtin, "Avtor i geroj v esteticheskoj dejatel' nosti" [Author and character in aesthetic activity]. In (42), pp. 7-180. Earlier partial publication in: *Voprosy filosofii* 7 (1977) and in *Voprosy literatury* 12 (1978). Written about 1922 to 1924.

4. M. Bakhtin, "Problema soderzhanija, materiala i formy v slovesnom khudozhestvennom tvorchestve" [The problem of content, material, and form in the verbal artistic creation]. In (41), pp. 6-71. Earlier partial publication in *Kontekst 1973.* Moscow, 1974. Written in 1924.

5. M. Bakhtin, "Iz lekcij po istorii russkoj literatury. Vjacheslav Ivanov" [Extracts from lectures on the history of Russian Literature. Viacheslav Ivanov]. In (42), pp. 374-83. Transcription by R. M. Mirkina, from a course taught in the 1920s, probably around 1924.

6. V. N. Voloshinov, "Po tu storonu social'nogo" [On this side of the social]. *Zvezda* 5 (1925):186-214.

7. V. N. Voloshinov, "Slovo v zhizni i slovo v poezii." *Zvezda* 6 (1926):244-67. Eng. trans. "Discourse in Life and Discourse in Poetry" to appear in *Writings by the Circle of Bakhtin.* Translated by Wlad Godzich. Minneapolis: Univ. of Minn. Press, forthcoming.

8. V. N. Voloshinov, *Frejdizm.* Moscow-Leningrad, 1927. Eng. trans. *Freudianism: A Marxist Critique.* Translated by I. R. Titunik. New York: Academic Press, 1976.

9. P. N. Medvedev, "Ocherednye zadachi istoriko-literaturnoj nauki" [The current tasks of a historical literary science]. *Literatura i marksizm* 3 (1928):65-87.

10. P. N. Medvedev. *Fromal'nyj metod v literaturovedenii* (Leningrad, 1928). Eng. trans. *The*

Formal Method in Literary Scholarship. Translated by A. J. Wehrle. Baltimore, Maryland: Johns Hopkins University Press, 1978.

11. V. N. Voloshinov, "Novejshie techenija lingvisticheskoj mysli na Zapade" [The most recent currents of linguistic thought in the West]. *Literatura i marksizm* 5 (1928).

12. V. N. Voloshinov, *Marksizm i filosofija jazyka*. Leningrad, 1929. Eng. trans. *Marxism and the Philosophy of Language*. Translated by L. Matejka and I. R. Titunik. New York: Seminar Press, 1973.

13. M. Bakhtin, *Problemy tvorchestva Dostoevskogo*. Leningrad, 1929. Eng. trans. *Problems of Dostoyevsky's Poetics*. Translated by W. W. Rotsel. Ann Arbor: Ardis, 1973. A new English translation, including new materials, is available in the Theory and History of Literature Series: *Problems of Dostoevsky's Poetics*. Edited and translated by Caryl Emerson with an introduction by Wayne C. Booth. Minneapolis: Univ. of Minn. Press, 1984.

14. M. Bakhtin, "Predislovie" (Preface). In L. N. Tolstoj, *Polnoe sobranie khudozhestvennykh proizvedenij*, vol. 11, "Dramaticheskie proizvedenija" [Dramatic works], pp. 3-10. Moscow-Leningrad, 1929.

15. M. Bakhtin, "Predislovie [Preface]. In Tolstoj, *Polnoe sobranie khudozhestvennykh proizvedenij*, vol. 13, "Voskresenie" [Resurrection], pp. 3-20. Moscow-Leningrad, 1929. Eng. trans. in *Writings by the Circle of Bakhtin*. Translated by Wlad Godzich. Minneapolis: Univ. of Minn. Press, forthcoming.

16. V. N. Voloshinov, "O granicakh poétiki i lingvistiki," in *V bor'be za marksizm v literaturnoj nauke*, pp. 203-40. Leningrad, 1930. Eng. trans. "On the Borders between Poetics and Linguistics," in *Writings by the Circle of Bakhtin*. Translated by Wlad Godzich. Univ. of Minn. Press, forthcoming.

17. V. N. Voloshinov, "Stilistika khudozhestvennoj rechi. 1. Chto takoe jazyk?" [Stylistics of artistic discourse: 1. What is language?]. *Literaturnaja uchëba* 2 (1930):48-66.

18. V. N. Voloshinov "Stilistika khudozhestvennoj rechi. 2. Konstrukcija vyskazyvanija." Eng. trans. "Stylistics of artistic discourse: 2. The Construction of Utterances," in *Writings of the Circle of Bakhtin*. Translated by Wlad Godzich. Minneapolis: Univ. of Minn. Press, forthcoming.

19. V. N. Voloshinov, "Stilistika khudozhestvennoj rechi. 3. Slovo i ego social'naja funkcija" [Stylistics of artistic discourse. 3. Discourse and its social function]. *Literaturnaja uchëba* 5 (1930):43-59.

20. P. N. Medvedev, *Formalizm i formalisty* [Formalism and the Formalists]. Leningrad, 1934.

21. M. Bakhtin, "Slovo v romane." In (41), pp. 72-233. Earlier partial publication in: *Voprosy literatury* 6 (1972). Written in 1934-1935. Eng. trans. "Discourse in the Novel," in *The Dialogic Imagination*, pp. 259-422. Edited by Michael Holquist, translated by Caryl Emerson and Michael Holquist, Austin, Texas: Univ. of Texas Press, 1981). *Dialogic Imagination* herafter cited as *DI*.

22. M. Bakhtin, "Roman vospitanija i ego znachenie v istorii realizma" [The novel of apprenticeship and its significance in the history of realism], pp. 188-236. Written in 1936-38.

23. M. Bakhtin, "Formy vremeni i khronotopa v romane." In (41), pp. 234-407. Earlier partial publication in: *Voprosy literatury* 3 (1974). Written in 1937-1938, except for "Concluding Remarks," Eng. trans. "Forms of Time and of the Chronotope in the Novel," in *DI*, pp. 84-258.

24. M. Bakhtin, "Iz predystorii romannogo slova." In (41), pp. 408-46. Earlier partial publication in : *Voprosy literatury* 8 (1965) and in *Russkaja i zarubezhnaja literatura*. Saransk, 1967. Written in 1940. Eng. trans. "From the Prehistory of Novelistic Discourse," in *DI*, pp. 41-83.

25. M. Bakhtin, *Tvorchestvo Fransua Rable i narodnaja kul'tura Srednevekovija i Renessansa*. Written in 1940 except for some additions. Eng. trans. *Rabelais and his World*. Translated by Helene Iswolsky. Cambridge, Mass.: MIT Press, 1968.
26. M. Bakhtin, "Rable i Gogol" [Rabelais and Gogol]. In (41), pp. 484-95. Earlier publication in: *Kontekst 1972*. Moscow, 1973. Written in 1940, revised in 1970.
27. M. Bakhtin, "Epos i roman." In (41), pp. 448-83. Earlier publication in: *Voprosy literatury* 1 (1970). Written in 1941. Eng. trans. "Epic and Novel," in *DI*, pp. 3-40.
28. M. Bakhtin, "K filosofskim osnovam gumanitarnykh nauk" [Toward the philosophical bases of the human sciences]. In (42), p. 409-11. Earlier partial publication in: *Kontekst 1974*. Moscow, 1975. Written about 1941.
29. M. Bakhtin, "Problema rechevykj zhanrov" [The Problem of the discursive genres]. In (42), pp. 237-80. Earlier partial publication in: *Literaturnaja uchëba* 1 (1978). Written in 1952-1953.
30. M. Bakhtin, "Problema teksta v lingvistike, filologii i drugikh gumanitarnykh naukakh. Opyt filosofskogo analiza" [The problem of text in linguistics, philology, and the other human sciences: An essay of philosophical analysis]. In (42), p. 281-307. Earlier publication in: *Voprosy literatury* 10 (1976). Written in 1959-1961.
31. M. Bakhtin, "K pererabotke knigi o Dostoevskom." In (42), pp. 308-27. Earlier publication in: *Kontekst 1976*. Moscow, 1977. Written in 1961. Eng. trans. "Toward a Reworking of the Dostoevsky Book." In *Problems of Dostoevsky's Poetics*, appendix II. Edited and translated by Caryl Emerson. (Minneapolis: Univ. of Minn. Press, 1984).
32. M. Bakhtin, *Problemy poetiki Dostoevskogo* [Problems of Dostoevsky's Poetics], 2nd ed. Rev. of (13). Moscow, 1963.
33. M. Bakhtin, "Pis'mo I. I. Kanaevu o Gëte" [Letter to I. I. Kanaev on Goethe]. In (42), p. 396. Written 11 October 1962.
34. M. Bakhtin, "Pis'mo I. I. Kanaevu o Gëte" (Letter to I. I. Kanaev on Goethe]. In (42), pp. 396-97. Written in January 1969.
35. M. Bakhtin, "Recenzija ma knigu L. E. Pinskogo *Shekspir*" [Review of *Shakespeare* by L. E. Pinski]. In (42), pp. 411-12. Written in 1970.
36. M. Bakhtin, "Otvet na vopros redakeii Novo go mira" [Response to the question of the editorial committee of *Novyj mir*]. In (42), pp. 328-35. Earlier publication in: *Novyj mir* 11 (1970).
37. M. Bakhtin, "O polifonichnosti romanov Dostoevskogo" [On polyphony in the novels of Dostoevsky]. *Rossija/Russia* 2 (1975):189-98. Earlier publication in Polish in: *Współczesność* 17-30 (October 1971). Interview from 1970 or 1971.
38. M. Bakhtin, "Iz zapisej 1970-71 godov" [Extracts from notes from the years 1970-71]. In (42), pp. 336-60.
39. M. Bakhtin, "Zakljuchitel'nye zamechanija" [Concluding remarks]. In (41), pp. 391-407. Conclusions to (23). Written in 1973.
40. M. Bakhtin, "K metodologii gumanitarnykh nauk" [Concerning methodology in the human sciences]. In (42), pp. 361-73. Earlier partial publication in: *Kontekst 1974*. Moscow, 1975. Written in 1974.
41. M. Bakhtin, *Voprosy literatury i éstetiki*. Moscow, 1975. Eng. trans. of four of the essays in *DI*.
42. M. Bakhtin, *Estetika slovesnogo tvorchestva* [The aesthetics of verbal creation]. Moscow, 1979. Published by S. G. Bocharov.
43. "M. M. Bakhtin i M. I. Kagan (po materialam semejnogo arkhiva)" [M. M. Bakhtin and M. I. Kagan, materials from family archives]. *Pamjat'* 4 (1981). Letters and documents edited by K. Nevel'skaja.

Index

Index

Closure, 66, 69
Cohen, Hermann, 3
Cohen, Jonas, 94
Collective memory, 73; in genre, 84
Communication: model of, 54, 55. *See also*
    Being
Completion (*zavershennost*), 53, 81-82, 99-
    100, 105
Consciousness, 94-112; authorial, 104, 105;
    plurality of, 104; unmerged, 104
Context of enunciation, 42-51 *passim*, 54,
    71; decisive role for meaning, 5, 26;
    frames text, 23; smell of, 56
Contextual harmonies, 57
Culture: dialogics of, 104; and exotopy,
    109-110; idealist, 105; popular vs. of-
    ficial, 78
"Current Tasks of Literary-Historical Schol-
    arship, The," 8

Death: as dialogical concept, 98
Defamiliarization (*stranenie*), 20
Descartes, Rene, 59
Dialect: as type of differentiation, 57; as
    verbal horizon, 20
Dialectic: and dialogue, 104
Dialogue, x, xi, xiii, 18, 22, 23, 51, 62; with
    author, 106; being exists only in, x, xi;
    and dialectic, 104; between discourses,
    44; interior, 70; of styles in epochs, 76;
    of texts, 38, 107; with third entity, 111
Dialogic (dialogical), 60-61; cleavage of, 64-
    65; the dialogical minimum, 21; inter-
    action of discourses, 66; and intertextual,
    48, 50; knowledge of the subject, 18; life
    as, 97; vs. logical, 61; vs. monologic, 63;
    relations of utterance, 49; understanding,
    16
Dialogism, 104-105; *in absentia/in praesen-
    tia*, 77-78, 87
Dilthey, Wilhelm, 16, 22, 28
Discourse, x, 24, 33, 39, 54, 56, 58, 61; ab-
    sence of answer in, 111; active vs. passive
    styles in, 70-72; authorial, 104; classifica-
    tion of representation of, 70; degree of
    presence of, 73; and dialogue, 60; in
    genres, 82-84; ideological, 102; inter-
    individual, 52; internal/external, 32;
    linear vs. pictural in, 68-69; locus of, 71-
    72; modalities of, 89; nature of, 111;
    objectal character of, 68, 71; organizes

object, 55; quoting vs. quoted, 68-69;
    reification of, 102; reported, 68; repre-
    sentation of, 68-74; responsible, 102;
    restriction of diversity in, 57; role in
    human sciences, 15; as scenario, 47;
    science of, 25; signification in, 30; social
    life of, 34; as three-role drama, 52; types
    of, 57; units of, 51
"Discourse in Life and Discourse in Poetry,"
    7, 41, 67
"Discourse in the Novel," 35, 57, 64, 71,
    74, 77, 91
Doctor Faustus, 111
Dogmatism: authoritarian, 75; rationalist, 75
Dostoevsky, Fyodor, x, 14, 33, 35, 66, 84,
    101, 106 *passim*; Bakhtin on, *see Prob-
    lems of Dostoevsky's Poetics, The*;
    heterogeneous nature of his characters,
    103; and man in capitalist society, 111;
    pluralistic world of, 104
*Dostoevsky and Sentimentalism. An Essay
    in Typological Analysis*, 6
Dramatic, the, 87, 89-90

Ego, 32. *See* Freud, Sigmund
Eikenbaum, Boris, 37, 38
Einfühlung, 22, 98. *See also* Empathy
Einstein, Albert, 14
Empathy, 98-99, 108; (*vchustvovanie*), 109
Energeia vs. ergon, 20
Engels, Friedrich, 44
Enthymeme, 41-42
Epic, the, 87-90
Eschenbach, Wolfram von, 92
Exotopy (*vnenakhodimost'*), xii, 99-103,
    106; principle of, 109
Experience, 84, 96; organized by expres-
    sion, 43
Expression: precedes experience, 43-44

Fabliau, 76
Fielding, Henry, 85
Form and content, x, 34-40
Formal Method in Literary Studies, The, 8,
    11, 34, 36, 38, 39
Formalism, 34; and narrow ideologism, 35
Formalism and the Formalists, 8
Formalist aesthetics, 37
Formalists, 67; Bakhtin's evaluation of, 9-
    10, 36-40; and communication, 55; and
    objective empiricism, 19-20; and relation

Tzvetan Todorov is Mâitre des Recherches at the
Centre National de la Recherche Scientifique in Paris
and has also taught in the United States. Several
of his books on literary and cultural theory have been
translated into English; among them are *Introduction
to Poetics* (Minnesota, 1981), *Theories of the
Symbol*, and *The Conquest of America.*

Wlad Godzich is professor of comparative literature
at the University of Minnesota, and co-editor,
with **Jochen Schulte-Sasse**, of the series Theory and
History of Literature.